UPON THIS
ROCK.

UPON THIS
ROCK.

THE THIRD "SEASON" OF
OUR FATHER'S EVANGELICAL CHURCH

BRAD BROWN

For information about this title or to order other books and/or electronic media, contact the publisher:

Brad A Brown
bradbrownauthor.com
BRADSLAND@aol.com

ISBNs:
979-8-9870461-6-6 (hardcover)
979-8-9870461-7-3 (softcover)
979-8-9870461-8-0 (eBook)

Printed in the United States of America

Cover and Interior design: 1106 Design

This book is dedicated to my grandparents,
Paul and Rae Brown, Elmer and Marjorie Winegar,
who took me in like no other grandson.
They became my foursome of guiding lights,
illuminating my past, present, and future.

Brad Brown
May 2004

Acknowledgments

As the fictional town of Monument gets more deeply rooted and more complicated, Dr. Brian Morrison has seen to it that its author has received the perfect balance of feedback, encouragement, and hope. Thanks, Brian, for being one of the rare individuals in my life who speaks "Brad." A big thank-you also to his wife, Annette, for "painting the town." My deepest appreciation to my dear friend Rick Johnson, who has been such a rock for me, especially as an author. To Jeanie Hamilton, Linda Osti, and Karen Voorhis; upon your expertise this book has been built. Lastly, to my wife and soul mate, Cindy, who has been God's messenger in rescuing me from certain "Colby Block" tendencies. And to Charissa and Courteney, the two most important people in the next generation, to whom this work will be handed down. May the passing of this book into your precious hands allow it the distinction of being not merely an aging hand-me-down but perhaps a flawed, timeless heirloom about the family—and their God.

— Brad Brown
September 2004

TABLE OF CONTENTS

Preface

"If history were taught in the form of stories,
it would never be forgotten."

—Rudyard Kipling

I have traveled around the globe from the comfort of my couch thanks to the literary travel agent known as historical fiction. I have devoured the great works of the master of the genre, James A. Michener, and his heir apparent, Edward Rutherford. I was captivated by James Clavell's six-novel *Asian Saga*. Also, honorable mention to Stephen Harrigan's *The Gates of the Alamo* (which provided background for portions of my second book, *Rightly Dividing?*). The very idea of fictional characters rubbing shoulders with historic figures, and fictional locations sharing the map with historic places makes a gripping merger by which we emotionally invest in an historical past that now jumps right off the page.

Hence, this book is uniquely structured as an historical novel. Instead of chapters, the story is divided into five major set pieces depicting the life and times of a quintet of fictional families who make up an integral part of the town of Monument and its one and only church. The sections are connected by "Interludes," which fuse together each dramatic exhibition.

Some insider information:

— The six cassette tapes that close out the Introduction are real. My paternal grandfather, Paul P. Brown, was the oldest living native of Burbank, California, for the last few years of his life. The Burbank Historical Society recorded his story "for the record." I was present during those recordings. It was 20 years later, however, before I listened to them for the very first time. I took copious notes and transposed my grandfather's memories from Burbank to Monument.

Colby Block now shares his history.

— Brown Lake, into which Cyril Holbert recklessly dives, is also real. It was named after one of my grandfather's brothers, Rollie Brown, who owned the lake, using it for irrigation purposes and the surrounding area to grow potatoes. This was before it became well known as Toluca Lake, now a private golfing sanctuary surrounded by a charming, opulent Southern California neighborhood.

— I actually participated in the Dixie Cup prank on a friend; was busted for my puppet parody of "Fritz 'n Fran"; fought Wes the mule to the bottom of the Grand Canyon; and rescued a beloved phonograph record from the bottom of our swimming pool.

These and other revelations are surrounded by the traditional pairing-up of the factual and the fanciful that make historical fiction such a powerful method of storytelling.

So enjoy this rambunctious retrospective populated by protagonists, antagonists, visionaries, villains, saints, soldiers, dignitaries, delinquents, and a whole host of everyday folks— probably in many ways not much different than your own immediate family and its ancestors.

For each of us, they are a cumulus cloud of witnesses that can bring thunder, lightning, welcome rain, or a spectacular sunset. An atmosphere from antiquity that begins guiding from above but eventually slides under our feet to become an assortment of foundations. The Third "Season" of Our Father's Evangelical Church chisels down *below* the human footprints to the One Foundation that not only supports us all but calls out,

"Don't just stand there—make history!"

—Brad Brown
January 2024

"All other ground is sinking sand."

—Edward Mote

INTRODUCTION

"A noise like the mournful call of a whale slowly rolled over the thick layer of clouds that blanketed the feisty little planet in an otherwise quiet solar system. Angelic beings cocked their ears, listened, and then shook their heads in disbelief. The Father was up to something, to be sure. The noise grew in intensity before it finally abated in a lingering rumble. 'So that was it,' the angelic and curious deduced from the diminishing vibrations underneath the entire celestial kingdom. The Dennis the Menace of the Milky Way had just crossed over the line. The pesky population inhabiting the blue, twirling ball was about to get another wake-up call. The planet's first wake-up call was resting comfortably on His Throne, over on the right. Cherubim and Seraphim immediately put their heads together and whispered their own brand of conjectures to one another. True facts began to come to the surface of the nervous and jittery twaddle and prattle humming up and down the rungs of Jacob's Ladder among the chattering ranks of the Father's second-most celebrated creations.

"The troublesome planet was the target—that was true enough. But it turned out to be much more specific than that. On one of the seven continents, one of the little countries that had been formed by the Father, for, by some unknown reason, His shedding His grace upon it, had been trying to squirm out of His grip for quite some time—by Earth's standard of time measurement, anyway. By the sound of the reverberating call, the enlightened angelic realm expelled a unanimous sigh of pity. This was the sound of the Father no

3

longer tightening His grip. He was marshaling His forces and slamming down His fist . . ."

"Well, how is it?" I looked up to see Maria staring at me, a tainted dust rag hanging limp and exhausted in her hand, the end result of the most recent dirt-drenched swipe across our fireplace mantle.

"So far, so good," I replied, "although I have only read the first page!" There was a slight tone of unintentional indignation in my voice. Maria had an uncanny knack for disturbing me the moment I sat down to read . . . anything. It might be her whispering under her breath, singing a quiet song supposedly to herself, or just circling around me, banging things together that did not require a collision, and making all kinds of unnecessary racket . . . just to make sure I knew that she was there!

I knew one thing for certain, *hamsters* knew that she was there!

When Maria was eight years old, she had a pet white hamster. Since it was on such a rare occasion that her hard-working-class parents would allow such diverting extravagances to infiltrate their rather regimented household, Maria doted on the creature with an exuberance of love and compassion—taking care of "Snowflake's" every want and need, including a sawdust-lined, plastic hamster hamlet, complete with spinning wheels to nowhere and multi-layered, sinuous freeways of colorful tubing through which the little, rambunctious rodent could explore. One day, when Snowflake was out and about on a scheduled field trip in Maria's room, it unexpectedly relieved itself, casting pellet-droppings on the carpet like brown, miniature hailstones. Nicole Ponticelli, while patrolling her daughters' bedrooms in the afternoon, poked her head through the doorway, spied the "accident" strewn across the floor and immediately required that Maria vacuum up the evidence.

Maria obediently retrieved the vacuum cleaner and, in no time, her bedroom was devoid of any further "residue." However, Snowflake had freely scampered by as she was finishing up, and Maria caught sight of one last, lingering pellet still attached to the hamster hindquarters from whence it came. Conveniently, since she still had the vacuum nozzle in hand, Maria leaned down and, like an accomplished proctologist, moved the stainless-steel anteater snout into position. Maria did not anticipate the inhaling efficiency of the appliance, and, with a sickening, split-second suction-slurp, the vacuum cleaner swallowed Snowflake whole!

Maria felt the upward bumping and jostling of her little pet catapulting through the hose, like a devoured mouse sliding down the gullet of a snake, and into the cylindrical body of the vacuum's main nerve center for the storing and breaking down of all things sucked. In a panic, Maria let go of the serpent's head and let out a scream. Her mother interrupted her patrolling to rush back into the room, ascertain the problem by reading Maria's stricken face, her pointing finger, and the vacuum cleaner still humming menacingly, hunkered-down, hose coiled, animate nozzle discreetly scanning the carpeted horizon for the next scurrying, incontinent gerbil.

Quick-thinking Nicole reversed the setting on the machine, blowing out all that had been recently gulped, shaking the hose coaxingly while hugging the overgrown dust buster in a makeshift Heimlich maneuver. A windswept Snowflake was eventually vomited out, tucking and rolling until the spinning revolutions left her in a listless, fuzzy white heap. Maria scooped up her hamstrung beloved pet, and with a few caresses and affectionate soothing, Snowflake regained consciousness. The trauma did, understandably, shorten its lifespan, but not before causing all of the pink ears throughout the four corners of Hamsterdam to now perk up in a panic at one deadly combination: the approach of Maria Ponticelli Block and the sound of a vacuum cleaner!

"I won't disturb you," she responded, picking up my feet off the coffee table and scouring the not-so-dusty surface under the shadow of my elevated, crossed legs. Not an avid reader herself (she read primarily for spiritual sustenance—her Bible, devotionals, Christian self-helps in times of questions or crises), she was still genuinely interested in the first published novel by our previous Senior Pastor, Milton Derringer, *Founding Fathers*.

I kept warily watching her fastidious annihilation of the invisible army of dust mites that had, presumably, set up camp on every flat surface of our living room.

"Well, go on!" she instructed.

But I was afraid to look down at page two. It would be a sure invitation that Maria could once again make her presence known. She was staring at me again, waiting for me to make the next move. I eyed her suspiciously. Slowly I began to lower my head, and finally my gaze, cautiously turning the page of *Founding Fathers* as I did.

"The streets of Washington, DC looked deserted in the crisp, winter dawn. The pulse-rate of the center of power had yet to make a blip on the world's screen. In a matter of moments, however, the streets would be abuzz with cars, buses, taxicabs, limousines, tourists, senators, congressmen, dignitaries, Secretaries of State, FBI agents—the coming dawn would begin in its usual blaze of glory, and

the warmth would melt the icy streets, rejuvenating the thoroughfares into a steaming grid of crisscrossed avenues, all leading into one another, and the United States federal government would leap into action once again, taking hold of the joystick that controlled the game for the only remaining world power."

"Ian, we really need to re-do the kids' rooms sometime this year."

". . . taking hold of the joystick that controlled the game for the only remaining—"

"Do you think we can take a Saturday and paint? I'll do the prepping. You can roll the ceilings, OK?"

I nodded indolently. *". . . taking hold of the joystick that controlled the game for the—"*

"O Worship the King, all glorious above," a singing whisper, floating unobtrusively into my left ear. Like Chinese water torture.

". . . taking hold of the joystick that controlled the game for—"

"It springs from the hills, it descends to the plains, and . . ." It was coming from the right now, from the direction of a not-so-dusty end table.

". . . taking hold of the joystick that controlled—"

"What do you want for dinner?"
I slammed the book shut.

"Peace and quiet!!" I said, after the CRACK! of my book-slamming had made my perturbations all the more obvious.

Maria didn't miss a beat. "Can't live on that," she said as she and her blackened dust rag glided out of the room.

Before she returned to shove the couch and its whiplashed occupant this way and that to the deafening drone of the vacuum cleaner, now yelling her songs as she pushed and pulled the contraption on its roaring dragnet of suction across the unsuspecting surface of forest-green carpet, I had a chance to observe the dust cover of Milton Derringer's first novel—his dream come true. The rather abstract cover of *Founding Fathers* featured an inviting snow-blanketed photograph of the Washington, DC Mall, facing the Capitol, taken with a fish-eye lens, as in a recently shaken snow globe. Within the circumference of the photograph were floating, falling-picture-pieces of stoic, bygone colonial-era faces appearing to have been ripped from that famous painting by John Trumbull depicting the Signing of the Declaration of Independence.

Congratulations, Milton, I thought to myself. He had really done it. He had realized his dream to write a novel. I'd been missing our Senior Pastor since he first left our shores to become a life insurance salesman in Tacoma, Washington. His absence was more acutely felt during the tumultuous years under Tony Meece—the Genghis Khan of the Good Book—who was now upbraiding his unsuspecting, weary congregation by spewing forth the sulfurous "scripture of bibliolatry" and dropping hermeneutic hydrogen bombs somewhere in mid-town Galveston, Texas.

I looked up to see the silhouette of Maria's head, now up inside a lampshade, batting the inside curvature with the vacuum nozzle in one hand, and, with her dust rag in the other hand, rubbing the light bulb like Aladdin's lamp.

8

Her grandfather, Vincenti Ponticelli, knew his wish had come true when his ship arrived at New York Harbor's Ellis Island in September of 1920. He was an immigrant from Pisa, Italy, where they had lived under the crooked shadow of the Leaning Tower. His family had come to seek a new life in America. After working ten years in the steel industry, Vincenti was hired in March of 1930 by Starrett Brothers & Eken, Inc. to help install the chrome-nickel steel from the 6th to 102nd floors in what would be the tallest building in the world, the Empire State Building. Two years after its completion, Vincenti sat in the darkened theater of Radio City Music Hall, watching King Kong climb—with Fay Wray in his hand—up the side of the very building he had helped erect. He sat there beaming with pride (while little children were running out of the theater in terror) that the building did not lean at all under the massive gorilla weight of the 8th Wonder of the World, not like that tilting tower in his own home country!

Vincenti succeeded as a talented steelworker and eventually moved his family to upstate New York. His son, Paulo, would continue the migration westward to California in 1961, where he would work tirelessly as a general contractor in order to support his wife, Nicole, and their two little daughters, Maria and Angela. Paulo's work ethic had been firmly ingrained in him ever since he had first heard the emotional description given him by his father from the railing of that ship more than 40 years earlier. "THERE IT IS!" Vincenti would shout while pointing his finger, eyes still welling up with appreciative tears, re-enacting that moment for his son when he had first caught a glimpse of the Statue of Liberty, her hammered-copper torch beckoning him with immovable light.

That same work ethic, dust rag and all, had obviously been passed down to his oldest daughter. But I thought the words inscribed on the plaque at the base of the Statue applied more accurately to her husband right about now!

Give me your tired, your poor,
your huddled masses yearning to breathe free,
the wretched refuse of your teeming shore.
Send these, the homeless, the tempest-tost to me.
I lift my lamp beside the Golden Door!

Three thousand miles from those inscribed words was my own lady liberty, my thorough spouse now scouring every square inch of our Promised Land on Chestnut Street. Watching her made me think of the synopsis I'd given last Sunday. Yes, under the softer, slower, simpler-shepherd management of our new Senior Pastor Roland Jeffries, my synopses had been reinstated as a legitimate teaching method.

Pastor Jeffries, by sharp contrast to his predecessor, actually lived up to his peaceful "pastoral" title. The only thing troublesome to me was his disproportionate love affair with choruses on Sunday mornings. He made sure that Troy Cobb included a hefty portion of them, while being careful to include the requisite throwing-of-the-hymn-bone for those more inclined to the staid and traditional. This hymn was usually sung while we were still seated at the beginning of the music portion of the service. It sounded as if it had been arranged by the local funeral parlor in Monument—just to make sure dusty and timeworn hymnology never found its way into the post-modern age with any sprucing up of its historic, musical character. The organ stops were set to imitate something out of *The Addams Family*, and we all joined in on the deliberate dirge, anxious for Hymn Halloween to be over. Then the giddy and exuberant worship team would run up to the platform, all ramped-up for the "real" worship to begin by chanting chorus after chorus after chorus after chorus after chorus. The congregation instantly was on its feet and stood there for what the more brittle, spirit-encrusted would call a "dog-and-pony show" for what seemed like days—days like a thousand years. Choruses were repeated over and over and over again, as if their lyrical substance would improve and deepen with age. But was this really fine wine, or was it just fast food? The younger crowd seemed to enjoy the repetition provided by this song service of spiritual senility. It was as if true worship could be conjured up only by the incantations of choruses, and not excavated from the memorabilia of hymns (although it seemed the increasingly rare occasion when any worship experience was ushered in from the spontaneous combustion of preconditioned hearts already on fire). In the meantime, we were all part of the ensemble cast of "Jericho: The Musical," repeating a chorus seven times in what seemed like as many days, hoping that the walls between ourselves and a real worship experience would finally come crashing down. After the eighth chorus, it wasn't walls that were crashing down—older folks could be seen dropping like flies, plopping back down into their seats, exhausted from the span of standing at attention. Then, like the spotting of an exotic animal on the African Veldt, there were even "sightings" of someone *really* worshiping—swaying with their hands actually in the air! This usually followed some swelling key change in the music, so the carefully listening spectators on the worship safari would be tipped off as to when to get out their binoculars and search for that all-too-elusive quarry: the worship call and celebration dance of charismatic, crooning bipeds.

The marriage between Mr. Traditional and Mrs. Contemporary was, indeed, a rocky one.

In spite of this, Pastor Jeffries lived up to his title and calling, clearly exemplifying his job description from Saint Paul's sizzling manifesto-missive to the province of Galatia, viewing each member of his congregation as a large-headed embryo needing to be born . . . again without any anesthesia other than the calming Spirit of God. Pastor Jeffries' empathy and intentionality writhes with pangs that produce each member. He is not satisfied until he can press his pudgy nose up to the window in the O.F.E. Maternity Ward and see row upon row of cooing, gurgling, smiling male and female little Christs that he himself had so painfully birthed.

I was doing a series in my fifth-grade Sunday school class, "Second to Nun," entailing events in the life of Joshua as recalled from his deathbed, in weekly haphazard flashbacks. It would be quite the understatement to say that it felt very, very good to be reciting, once again, my opening paragraph to my new fifth-graders, this time from Joshua, Chapter Seven.

"Big, black Achan was the original Thieving Magpie. He could not resist swooping down and grabbing in his crooked beak shiny objects that he had espied from his perch high aloft in the Magpie Tree. Soon he began taking anything and everything that did not belong to him, shiny or not. When it came time for the 3,000-member magpie flock to overthrow and occupy a much better and taller grove of trees inhabited by predatory vultures, big, black Achan decided to keep the abandoned vulture leftovers

that he found in his new nest. The crowded branch began to bend precariously under the weight of old bones, rotten fruit, and the soon-to-be hatching vulture eggs that big, black Achan was sitting upon. As a result, a total of 36 fellow magpies slid off the sagging limb and fell to the ground far below. As soon as the secret 'collection' of big, black Achan was discovered, he was thrown out of the tree, and the once-drooping branch sprang happily back into place."

After much forward-and-reverse jerking motion, my traveling couch made its final approach and came in for an abrupt landing back in front of the coffee table, my knees pinched in-between. The crash test had not gone well. My knuckles were white from holding on to the padded arm and seat cushions. Throw pillows had lived up to their name, and I needed a chiropractor. I was about to make my harrowing test-pilot experience known to Mrs. Mission Control, when cleaning-machine Maria—a combination of Proverbs 31 and some really strong Italian espresso—snapped off the vacuum cleaner switch and announced that she was going to the store.

My pitiful request for an aspirin was lost to the slam of the front door. When the rise and fall of our Honda Accord's engine had sufficiently faded down Chestnut Street to indicate enough distance had been traversed, I opened Milton's book a second time, scanning page two for the last line of memory.

". . . taking hold of the joystick that—"

RATTATTATTATTATTATTATTATTAT TATTATTATTATTAT!

Work had resumed. The jackhammers were back. I gave my look of anguish and defeat to the oval mirror on the opposite side of the fireplace mantle. It seems our house on Chestnut Street was perfectly placed in the path of traveling sound waves as they ferociously carried themselves down the canyon and vibrated our house with every tap of a hammer, chink of a chisel, bawl of a workman, rap of a hard hat, roar of a sandblaster, or . . . the rattle of a jackhammer.

The City Council of Monument had made a valiant effort to start the work in honor of the city's 75th anniversary. But the dense bureaucratic jungle of red tape, permits, zoning ordinances, contractor bids, environmental-impact reports, and a unanimous-vote requirement that did not exist in 1922 had forestalled the project for a couple of "these things take time" years.

RATATATATATATATATATATATATAT ATATATATATATAT!

I put down my book and looked out the front window to the northwest at what looked like a large white plume of smoke that was billowing upward in the distance, like the last gasp of a raging hillside fire when finally doused with water. I actually smiled at the sensations. These were sights and sounds not seen or heard in these parts for more than 80 years. Not a living soul was around who remembered that first ordeal. But it had given our town distinction.

It had given our town its name.

High up on our mountainside, "The Sheik" was emerging. The head of Rudolph Valentino was being uncovered and . . . finished!

Yes, the *right* side of the movie star's face was actually being called forth from the blank slate of granite. Through the extraordinary process of granite-grafting, Rudolph's left ear was completely whole once again, and the restored tip of his nose seemed to protrude right off the silver screen. His Arab headdress had also been dug out and polished up to its full Middle-Eastern luster.

The right side was progressing nicely. Most all of the features were distinguishable. Crowds gathered at the base of the mountain (where the view of the head seemed monstrous), sitting on the makeshift grandstands that had been erected for the forthcoming dedication ceremony, right next to Our Father's Evangelical Church. Once again, traffic was congested on the freeway at the bottom of the hillside, due to "spectator slowing."

However, the consistent dust clouds of granite unleashed from the mountainside covered the quaint habitats of the foothills with a thick coating of white. Houses nestled in this corridor looked like Pompeii villas in 79 AD at the base of Mount Vesuvius, when the first blast of that famous volcano sent many feet of settling ash in every direction—from Oplontis to Herculaneum. During these months, there was no keeping up with the granite powder. Like seams having been ripped open in a vast pillow fight between the gods, it seeped under doorways and windowsills and attached itself to shirt sleeves and pant legs with equal tenacity. It slipped under the soles of shoes and lodged itself in the maze of tread, only to be released when the better offer of shining plush carpet was underfoot.

On many days when asphyxiation threatened, handkerchiefs and bandanas were seen covering the noses and mouths of the townsfolk, making a good portion of the population look like they were from the Old West, each planning to rob our local bank at the same time.

All this accounts for Maria's militant battle on the side of cleanliness. Undaunted, she. Like a Depression mom in the Dust Bowl of Oklahoma, she whipped her dust rag and blasted Lemon Pledge at those insidious particles waiting to take up residence on any inviting surface, dancing in the sunlight that was streaming through the window. We were the typical nuclear family with the mushroom cloud to prove it.

It is a fair price to pay, I thought as I continued staring at the nearly completed face on the mountainside. To think that the head of Rudolph Valentino was actually going to be finished in my lifetime! I was not the only one to wax nostalgic. Many people in town were looking up at the flurry of activity on the mountainside and doing the same type of pondering about our past, our present, and our future.

At the coming of my 46th birthday, this put me in a far more prevalent state of bygone-days preoccupation than usual. This would be the basis upon which I would request my party to include yet another tour of the Monument Museum by none other than their very best docent, my father, Seth Block. He and my mother had agreed to my birthday request and drove down from their beachfront condo up north to blow the dust off (which you could do literally these days!) my father's memorized museum speech, which he had recited hundreds of times to as many rapt tourists when he had lived in our town.

Their excursion southward, however, was to serve a dual purpose for my 75-year-old father, as it would also give him a much-needed respite from the complicated church polity he had found himself enmeshed in as a deacon newly out of mothballs at his local church. It had been a while since he had last served so faithfully at Our Father's Evangelical Church, and he had enjoyed the rest and blissful ignorance that comes from not knowing all of the inside workings of a church and its leadership. But the congregation had persistently asked him to serve on their Board year after year. After he felt he had been away long enough, he had finally acquiesced. But he was worried. Of this, he spoke in harsher terms to my mother than his church leadership memories would have justified.

"I don't know if I have the stamina anymore to crush any organized resistance, or enough patience with those younger crew members that make up a present-day Deacon Board."

The consistent clinking and clanging of church machinery brought him right back to the grindstone as he and his fellow deacons, clad in spiritual overalls, frantically raced to every source of shrill, metallic noise to oil the cogs and grease the gears and bearings so that the nuts and bolts would purr more often than they would squeal. This had eaten up his seemingly brief time of rest within moments. For better or worse, the church was an unchanging institution. "You pick right up where you left off!" he would say to my mother as he dragged himself over the threshold of their condo after a deacon meeting that had labored into the wee hours of the next day.

So both he and my mother were more than willing to fly like birds as far south as their car would carry them. And my 46th birthday was the perfect excuse to see their two sons and three grandkids, and get reacquainted with many of their old friends in Monument. It would also give them a chance to see the much-lauded progress of Rudolph Valentino, photos of which had made their way even into the local newspaper adorning their condo coffee table from time to time.

I invited Lorne and Candice Carlson to come along, and Dennis and Patty O'Conner to also drive down from their northerly abode and accompany our family on our excursion through the halls of history that the Monument Museum had so faithfully preserved.

So, on the Saturday afternoon of my birthday, we ventured forth to the Monument Museum.

We were greeted by Sara Pollard, the curator, who gave my father and mother a big "welcome home" hug. She smiled broadly as she pinned an "Official Docent" badge to my father's blazer with joyful satisfaction and due pomp and ceremony. And we were off. My dad was back to his old self as he raised his hand

and led the large pack of Blocks (myself, my mother, Maria, Sharayah, Samantha, Owen, Penny, and Owen, Jr., who seemed to be less inclined to display hysterical struggles for power as he grew older), along with the four representatives of Carlsons and O'Conners, through the first floor of the museum.

Thanks to a generous cadre of donors and some shrewd financial investing by the Board of Directors, the Monument Museum had been completely refurbished some years before— from niche to Newell post—and now included some breathtaking and eye-catching artifacts.

The entryway into the museum was a series of colorful tents, flags, awnings, and palm trees right out of an Arab desert encampment, only here there were dozens of bright movie lights beaming down from scaffolding above, and, situated throughout this exterior "set," amidst coiled wires and cables, were empty "director's" chairs, with names like Agnes Ayers, Walter Long, and Rudolph Valentino printed across the canvas backrests. The three-story wall facing the parking lot of the museum was completely covered in plaster rock formations depicting the Arabian Desert, giving one the complete feeling as you walked over the beds of trucked-in sand that you were actually entering Hollywood, circa 1921.

The first floor, with its vaulted ceiling, housed the larger displays. In the center of the room was an actual cable car from "The Funicular" system, sister to the Angels Flight cars that were going up and down Los Angeles' Bunker Hill at the same time in history. "The Funicular" of Monument carried passengers up and down the hillside, tracing the same route as present-day Valentino Avenue, starting at First Street at the bottom of the hill, present-day Max Stellar Boulevard. You could actually climb aboard the display car and pretend you were a passenger from the past going up and down the bustling street of a very young town.

In a far corner was a diorama housing a gigantic chunk of granite appropriated from the 1971 Sylmar Earthquake that had shaken off the tip of Rudolph Valentino's nose. It was placed in front of a floor-to-ceiling mural showing a distant view in perspective of the half head of Rudolph, a small, shadowy crater where the tip of his nose had been. Strewn about the dirt floor were hundreds of granite chunks of all shapes and sizes. When you stood at the railing of the exhibit, you felt like you were at the bottom of the mountain moments after the violent shaking of the ground underneath you had stopped and the tip of Rudolph's nose had come to a crashing halt. As with most multi-generational tours through museums, the younger ones just "oooooh'd and ahhhhh'd," while we "older folks" still shuddered from the memories firmly implanted on that fateful morning.

To one side of the exhibit was a large black-and-white blown-up photograph that looked like it could have been snapped from the shutter of Ansel Adams. It was a profile of Rudolph's nose taken from high up in the air with the camera facing west. Dangling precariously from a rope was the silhouette of Max Stellar in the process of "honeycombing," or smoothing out the tip. You could see the sun setting on the Pacific Ocean in the distance.

In an opposite corner was a second diorama, depicting a detachment of flag-bearing, armor-clad Conquistadors and Explorers, their backs to us, looking into a spectacular mural of the Pacific Ocean. The plaque on the railing relayed a brief history of the Spanish discovery of "Vista Pacifica," the first name of our beloved town.

The walls of the first floor were plastered with hundreds of photos, flags, and weapons. Glass cases lined the perimeter, filled with swords, guns, pottery, and old money. Off to one side was an old farm wagon, loaded down with a sumptuous mound of fake plastic watermelons, and hitched to a life-sized stuffed horse, ready to make the dusty journey over the mountain to the market in Los Angeles, just after the turn of the *previous* century. Adjacent were treasures of arcane farming machinery, a display of rusty barnyard behemoths, relics dug up from a bygone Jurassic John Deere agricultural eon now buried deep underneath our modern city: a tractor, a hay baler, a buck rake, with its 18-inch sharp metal teeth pointing menacingly like a giant bear claw—man's hardware advances in the "sowing and reaping" department. There was even a large garage-like room off to the side that housed a pantheon for car enthusiasts. It included a full-sized, old-fashioned Chevron gas station with two pump islands, around which were parked dozens of restored-to-perfection antique motor cars, from Models A to T, Bentleys to Edsels, all with the dazzling chrome and luxuriant upholstery of spit-and-polish mint condition.

This was topped off with an historically educational playroom for the kids, featuring a miniature, kiddie soundstage complete with rows of hanging costumes for dressing up and experiencing firsthand the glitz and glamour of Hollywood's golden age; a play farmhouse and barn with all of the plastic accessories, tools, hardware, and tractors for pretending rugged ranch life in "Vista Pacifica's" late 1800s; and a gigantic plaster facsimile of a mug from old Rudy's Malt Shop, into which they could tumble by sliding down an enlarged red-and-white-striped straw onto the milk chocolate-colored foam padding inside.

It took us more than an hour to finally make our way to the second floor, where many of the exhibits fell under the rubric of "Wars and Rumors of Wars," which was home to the much-anticipated World War I exhibit. My father still got choked up when he launched into the speech about his own father's tour of duty in France. I am not sure if this was the result of the refurbishment or just the fermentation of my aging imagination, but this time the mannequin standing at attention wearing Colby Block's original World War I army uniform seemed to look just like him as well. The verisimilitude was uncomfortable at first; I felt its glass eyes looking back at me. But the longer I stood there, listening to docent son reverently speak about deceased father, I began to feel a strange connection. My father stood next to the exhibit and gave us the background of this particular episode in Monument's history, which digressed into a personal look at the life and times of Colby Block. I had heard my father's speech at this juncture of the museum tour many times before. But this time it was different. More often than not, conjecture bowed to factuality. The players in these stories were much more well-rounded. Details were more vivid, and the scenes created in our minds as a result were colorful . . . and real! It was as if my father had discovered some new source material or something.

Returning to our home that night, after cake, ice cream, and the 12-member choir singing "Happy Birthday to You," I opened my birthday presents. They were the usual battery of requested literary works (always looking for an excuse to "buffet my body" with vocabulary), CDs, and clothes.

At the last, my father handed me a wrapped gift he had been furtively holding the entire evening. The colorful balloon birthday paper, once torn asunder, revealed a neat stack of six Memorex cassette tapes. I eyed him curiously.

My father began to explain, with great emotion, that since Colby Block had been the oldest living native of Monument for the last few years of his life, the Monument Historical Society had taken it upon itself to conduct a series of interviews with him, asking him questions about his life and the beginnings of the town of Monument. They had had the good sense to record these interviews on the most modern method available at the time, cassette tape.

In my hand were those tapes.

I looked up at my father, incredulous. He looked back, and our watering eyes spoke deeply in that father-son non-verbal moment, the patriarchal passing of some unspoken masculine baton.

The balance of the night was lightened by time spent casually chatting with one another (my brother Owen and Penny had to leave early, however, as Owen Jr. decided loudly that he did, in fact, want to overthrow his parents and their overblown, unnecessary discipline of him).

I remained somewhat preoccupied, however, and stole a glance every chance I could at those stacked cassette tapes now sitting on the living-room end table. What treasures did they reveal about my grandfather? How would I feel about audibly hearing his voice for the first time in more than 20 years? My father had confessed to me that it had been very difficult to listen to them at first, but, after a few moments, he found himself removed from the present, transported back to another time and place by the familiar but gruff voice of the oldest living native of Monument.

When our guests had departed, I began a top-to-bottom, needle-in-a-haystack search of our house on Chestnut Street for the only means of channeling the spirits of antiquity—a cassette player!

Miraculously, I found one in the attic. I did nothing more than bring it downstairs, set it next to the six cassettes on the end table, plug it in, load in cassette number one, and left it for an appropriate time in the future.

Now it seemed I was making a habit of staying up late on my birthdays, long after everyone had gone to bed, pondering into the night how well I had done with the life I had been served these past 46 years. Once I had given myself a passable grade, I decided the coast was clear to sneak in a few pages of *Founding Fathers*. I quietly slid the book toward me from where it was lying on the coffee table, somehow thinking the very swishing sound might wake Maria upstairs and she would come barreling down with a bucket and mop.

I opened to where I had last read. The signers of the Declaration of Independence had just appeared suddenly around present-day Washington, DC. I thought this would be welcomed escapism, but instead it brought back the full force of my father's birthday present to me.

". . . Forefathers appearing out of nowhere—coming from everywhere, their infiltration betraying a strategy by a greater Mastermind who knew enough to use those who would know the drill: re-establish the foundations, colonize the modern-day mind, and teach these upstarts a history lesson they will not soon forget.

"Original bodies now reunited with the actual voices and emotions from the past. Living, breathing reminders of where we had been and where we were going . . ."

I shut the book. Sighing to myself in surrender, I got up from the couch and walked over to the end table. I looked down at the cassette player, hesitating for only one brief moment before I pushed PLAY.

BLOCK

"ADAM! ADAM!" she called, exasperated, putting her hands above her eyes to shield her from the white heat of a blinding sun that had taken center stage in the middle of an extended, unending sky. The rolling, green Missouri hillocks, curled up in a fetal position, kept their backs to her cries. The tall bluegrass that covered their shoulders blew ripples like nervous, twitching muscles. The breeze, the birds chirruping in the distance, and beyond that, silence. The rhythms of the natural world betrayed an indifference to her plight. Everything would keep plodding along; sun, moon, stars, seasons—making the case of this missing boy very insignificant in the eyes of horizons that she was straining now to decipher. Sensing futility, she stormed back into the cabin.

"Wake up, Pete! Adam's gone!"

Her groggy husband stirred from the bed shoved into the far corner of the cabin. He had been lying on his side, facing the wall, the hairs on his shirtless back fluttering like the bluegrass on the hills that had ignored her optical pleas just moments before. She would not be ignored twice. "PETE!"

Pete sat up languidly and rubbed his eyes in a dreamy state of stupefaction. "What is it?"

"Adam's gone!"

"Probably went fishin'," he posited groggily.

"No." Mother's intuition. It had sprung from the vituperative conversation the night before when she had snapped. She would not lose her boy. No, sir. Not for this! As a matter of fact, according to her, there was no cause in the world worthy enough for her to unclench her maternal fingers from around the strapping young man who had sat red-faced across the rough-hewn pine table, the one whom she had cradled and nursed so peacefully sixteen short years before. "Mother, I have to go!" Adam had said. After a half hour of polite dinner conversation, he had floated the subject of the Northern army's desperate need for more manpower up to the table surface as gently as possible. It exploded like a soap bubble in his face when his mother recognized his intent.

"Your father needs you here. We cannot run this farm without you. Without families running farms, the country is nothin'."

"Mother, I am the only one left in this county my age who has not enlisted in the Army!" Adam tried desperately to portray a proper combination of passion and respect.

His mother brandished a spoon at him from her side of the table. "You are willing to desert our farm and all we have worked for to go and get yourself kilt!"

"The country is fallin' apart, and the Rebels must be stopped. The President even said that a house divided against itself cannot stand for very long. I want to do my part. Can't you see that?" Here Adam looked at his father to help champion his cause. He received only the top of his balding head, as his father kept his eyes looking down, mechanically stirring his pewter bowl of beef stew.

"An' you're willin' to split up this family so you can go fire a gun at some stranger?"

Adam nodded, his confidence unshakable.

"By the way, young man, it was Jesus who talked about that there house being divided. Lincoln was only quoting Holy Scripture!"

"You see, Mother—the Bible is even on my side."

"The Bible does not take your side, boy; there is only one side—God's!" His mother's eyes widened with rage as she hissed these words back to her only son.

"And He said you should not kill!"

"Killin' may be the only way to free the slaves. Look at all the death that had to happen so that Moses could get the Children of Israel out of Egypt. That was slavery, too, wasn't it?"

His mother's nightly lessons with her son through the Bible, starting before he could talk and walk, were now coming back to haunt her in the argumentation of her very bright 16-year-old, now exhibiting all of the characteristics of a restless young man.

"Reno is still workin' their farm." Adam's father had stirred his thin stew into a whirlpool of meat and vegetables, and finally joined in the conversation from a few sentences previous.

"Reno is . . ." Adam was about to argue the point about his spineless neighbor—boyhood chum Reno Devonshire—but thought better of it. He went back to his original point. "This is just like Egypt, mother."

"THIS IS NOTHING LIKE EGYPT, ADAM!" His mother had lost it. Snapped. Whether her reasoning now was foolproof or riddled with holes no longer mattered. Contentions were all neatly swept up into the great dustbin that closes the lid on all further discussion: "I am your mother, and you'll do as I say!"

End of story, biblical or otherwise.

To which Adam slammed down his spoon and stormed outside.

Ruth stood up to call him back, but Pete intervened. "He needs to cool off, dear. Let him be for a spell." She sat back down. Her husband was right. It would take an opinionated, wound-up personality such as Adam quite some time to "cool off," as he was his mother's son. She needed time to compose herself as well.

The two of them continued eating in awkward silence, each in their own way, chasing elusive wisdom, pondering the next move in the proper parenting of a headstrong boy about to explode upon the brink of manhood.

Adam did not come back to finish his dinner. He did not come back to apologize. He did not come back to say "good-night" or to say that he was going to sleep in the barn tonight.

He did not come back at all.

"Like I said, he's probably fishin'," Pete repeated the next morning while rubbing the sleep from his eyes, trying to obviate his wife's brewing panic.

With her hands on her hips, Ruth put an end to his wishful thinking.

"Wallace is missing, too!"

Pete blanched and looked up, now instantly awake. There was no need to take the horse. The lake was within walking distance. Adam had brooded over family arguments before. Adam had slept in the barn before. Adam had even missed breakfast the following day to make his point before. But this felt different. He had never taken his horse. It had never been like this.

Pete was on his feet in an instant, hopping toward the front door, hiking up his pants and snapping suspenders in the process. A few moments later he was back, winded and sweating in spite of the coolness of the early morning hour. "The cows haven't been milked! The saddle 'n tack's gone!" he pronounced, ashen-faced.

They both flew about the cabin, looking for clues.

"Food's been taken!" yelled Ruth to her husband, who was up in the loft. This was Adam's room, which revealed more evidence that this episode was reaching a terrifying conclusion.

Stunned, Pete mumbled under his breath, perhaps subconsciously to protect his dyspeptic wife, or at least to forestall the inevitable.

"Some of his clothes are gone. His rifle is gone. Good God. He's really gone and done it!"

Mother's intuition again. "Yes, he has!" she answered. She sat down at the table, the last place from which her son had been seen and heard, and cried the tears of war.

Eighteen months later, on April 25, 1865, Adam Block was spotted from the porch by his pining mother, limping over the bluegrass horizon. She assumed the role of the prodigal's father and ran to her son, embracing him, holding him up as she guided him back to the cabin, yelling for Pete to kill the fatted calf, Adam's apology falling upon forgiving, deaf ears. His face was worn, haggard by not only the horrors of war, but also by disillusionment.

He had snuck away in the dark on a morning that seemed like ages ago, anxious to be part of the righteous army with its righteous cause that would trample out the vintage where the grapes of wrath were stored. Instead, too many lost comrades, too many torn limbs, too many screams in the night from the makeshift infirmary, and the higher calling seemed less divine and more deranged with each passing week.

In the summer of 1864, Adam had been dispatched to Washington, DC, where, under the command of General Lew Wallace, he was to help stave off a Rebel attack on the capital city. Just prior to the arrival of the desperately needed reinforcement troops sent by Ulysses S. Grant, Adam was grazed by a Confederate cannonball at Monocacy that was not slowed by the splitting in half of a tree, but came barreling like a fiery comet to put Adam out of commission. His fate would have been more final had it not been for the quick thinking of Jubal Roth, a large black private lying next to him on the battlefield who grabbed Adam like a rag doll before the leaden sphere of death could mow him down. As a result, only his right leg had been stung, side-swiped by the meteoric projectile as it roared past them both like a bullet before shaking the earth when it exploded into a choking cloud of dirt and noxious smoke some 50 yards away.

Adam was laid up in an infirmary tent for nearly a week. The overworked and overwhelmed on-site doctor said that, in his professional opinion, Adam's leg would fully heal but warned that he would be limping for a time. Adam would not be able to participate in the squelching of post-war pockets of rebellion that would ignite from outposts and camps. He received honorable-discharge papers on the day President Abraham Lincoln was gunned down at Ford's Theater, and arrived back home to his mother's arms in Missouri on the day the President's assassin, John Wilkes Booth, received from the gun of a Union soldier the same fate that he himself had inflicted upon the Commander-in-Chief. The grueling odyssey back home had not only tired him, but among his other contusions and suppurated lacerations, had exacerbated the bruised leg bone and inflamed the surrounding tissue. The relapse laid him up for a few weeks in the cabin, in the bed downstairs. Aside from his mother's tireless, poultice-packing, 'round-the-clock care, neighbors also came to pay a call on the "Civil War Hero" whose sacrifice had won the war—or so the rumor had spread around the surrounding county. "It was merely a coincidence of timing," was Adam's explanation and plea (knowing deep within the recesses of his reasoning that his life had been spared by a much greater, guiding Hand who had seen fit to divert that cannonball instead of dispatching his soul, "harmlessly" shoving it into a divinely ordained mound of dirt). But this failed to quell the awe and reverence that emitted from all those who came to call during his mother's prescribed visiting hours, and who brought plates of cookies, tureens of soup, or just handfuls of fresh flowers.

One such supplicant was none other than the little sister of his neighbor Reno, Ruby Devonshire. He and Reno had always endured a strained, sometimes stormy relationship, which was now compounded by the schism of their individual responses to the War. But they had played civilly from time to time during their childhoods, hunting, fishing, and swimming together. Sometimes Ruby would insist on coming along, and sometimes parental edicts would force them to take her. This only added to their irritation at this parasitical little girl who was constantly asking questions of them or threatening to "tell on them" about their latest exercise in misbehavior to either set of parents.

But the chasm of age had closed while Adam had been away. Along with the rest of them, Ruby had aged 18 months as well, but her encounter with the clock had repackaged her into a beautiful, mature girl, someone who had caught the eye of the outstretched invalid on the bed in the cabin-fevered corner. But the eye-catching seemed to be mutual. The "girl next door" paid her respects to the young man with the gimpy leg far more frequently than his physical therapy required.

Within a few weeks, Adam Block and his neighbor Ruby Devonshire were a known item around the contiguous farms. Pete and Ruth were delighted and relieved on three fronts. First, to have their son returned to them whole from the vicious War Between the States, second, to once again have Adam's help beating swords into plowshares with the back-breaking work required to keep their farm treading water, and, lastly, to have such a sweet girl as Ruby Devonshire gracing their cabin so often.

Although he would not say clearly, it seemed that Adam *was*, in fact, smitten by this gorgeous girl, her deep-brown eyes and dark locks of black hair still contributing to a portrait of loveliness, even when Ruby was caked from head to toe with a dirt/perspiration mix while she attended to her own set of grueling chores on her adjacent family farm.

Winter, spring, summer, and harvest entered and exited for four rotations, their meteorological characteristics predicted by the farmer's Bible, the Almanac, to be favorable and, ultimately, bountiful. This proved to be true not only for crops but for courtships as well, in particular, that of Adam Block and Ruby Devonshire. When Adam was hugging her, he felt as if he was in the center of the universe. There was no place on Earth he'd rather be. However, in their fifth year together, like weather patterns cycling from sunny to inclement, the relationship between Adam and Ruby showed signs of wear and tear. Adam's detached nature and the privatization of his emotions became a most insurmountable hill. Ruby was a natural at leading the way in divulging her deepest feelings to this handsome farm boy. But as the relationship deepened, the extent to which Adam would reciprocate was in sharp contrast. Alas, he was simply incapable. Ruby tried everything in her power to draw him out. He was more comfortable with her than with any other person in his social circles. He had told her as much. But there was a secret place in the oceanic recesses of his heart, soul, and mind beyond which their bond was not permitted to trespass.

"Adam, talk to me!" Ruby would plead on the occasions when it was very apparent something was troubling him. The chase was on.

"Can't you see I'm tryin' to?" He would choke, losing his footing and his intonations betraying supreme discomfort. "I just don't want to hurt you."

"Your not talkin' hurts me more. Don't you trust me?" She would hold his head and look right into his eyes, a pursuit he loved and hated at the same time. He could keep eye contact with her for only so long.

And, after all these years, she would only chase him for so long.

"I'm fine. Really, I'm fine. Can't we talk about something else?" He had hung his head back down and gave her his helpless cue that he could not form into words whatever was going on in his head and heart.

After so many of these fruitless quests toward transparency, the time she would wait patiently for him to respond further grew shorter and shorter. She would sigh, disappointedly, and slowly take her hands out of his clasp. She, too, would have her head down as she turned and walked back down the path to her farm, thinking as she went that the enormous investment of time, energy, and emotion on her part was paying paltry dividends.

She knew Adam was straining with everything inside him to communicate and thus release himself from the bondage of fear, embarrassment, and inhibition, but the male role models before him had been clear and precise. Men who till and prepare the soil so that it will produce fruit do not have time to cultivate their hearts to do the same. Consequently, their souls get so hard and crusty over the years that no feminine spade can penetrate to break up the stubborn topsoil. Adam's friendship with his Creator was also under a similar lock and key. His vertical lines of communication were quite intimate, but unpacking the complexities of that relationship to anyone on a horizontal level was another thing entirely.

Had she looked back from walking home on this particular evening, she would have seen Adam slam his fist into the side of the barn, in response to what they both knew intuitively: even though he loved her, he was losing her.

It seemed the entire county shook their heads in disappointment when the relationship was terminated and Ruby went away to school. A few years later, the Devonshire farm was sold, as it was becoming too hard to maintain (son Reno was *not* interested in the work!). They moved to the city, and Ruby was married shortly thereafter.

Regret for this would track Adam Block for the rest of his life. But it would be coupled with a new resolve; He swore before God to never let a girl such as Ruby Devonshire ever slip through his terrified fingers again.

In 1875, he got his chance with Emiline Brody.

She was the complete opposite of the exquisite and probing Ruby Devonshire. Emiline was blond, short, stocky, and determined to get a man! What was a relief for Adam was that her self-sufficiency all too often belayed any snooping around his inner sanctum. She seemed to enjoy Adam, admired him as a dedicated, hard worker, and did not seem to mind his laconic attempts at meaningful conversation. As she was a full ten years younger than he (which he only discovered later, as she looked much older than in actuality), perhaps he thought she was just too young to know any better! Regardless, he was determined to give her more of himself than he had with Reno Devonshire's little sister. Whenever he would take these risks of self-disclosure with Emiline, they had always been met with warmth and admiration, with the full knowledge that the courage he had mustered in this regard had been far greater than any he had gathered for the attempted Rebel siege in Washington, DC.

Around the age of 28, Adam was married to Emiline. He continued working the farm, hiring more and more helping hands as his aging parents were able to work it less and less. He vowed to provide for his mother and father in reciprocation for all that they had done for him. This was an additional subconscious benefit, as their presence in the cramped quarters provided a secondary shield from intimate conversations. It was here that Emiline's determination showed astounding creativity, even to the amazement of their nosy, speculating neighbors. Somehow, some way, six children were born to Adam and Emiline over the next ten years. This was not counting a few miscarriages and two stillborns. In 1876, Adam, Jr. took up residence. In 1877 daughter Felicia graced the farm. In 1879, Pete came on-board. In 1881, Paul was added. In 1882, Maggie. 1883, Thomas.

The little cabin was expanded at the north and west ends to accommodate cribs and beds. Adam and Emiline occupied the loft, while his parents slept in the corner downstairs. Getting up in the morning and going to bed at night were becoming quite an experience in the Block household, along with everything in-between; meals, chores, and play. Even more of an experience was the Block family walking to, from, and marching down the aisle of the local church on Sunday mornings to take their seats in the pew. Their dominating an entire row was the least of Reverend Woodley's worries. Rather it was Adam, Jr. making Paul laugh uncontrollably during the prayer, or Pete jerking the pigtails of either Felicia or Maggie, and Thomas suddenly wailing for no apparent reason during the sermon, that worried him.

In spite of this, all felt it was a delightful, fulfilling time for three generations to grow and to grow up with one another.

After his parents had passed away, Adam grew weary with the farm of his childhood. He and Emiline decided to embark upon a grand adventure and move the entire brood to California!

In 1885, their Missouri land was sold, and their wagons were packed. The Block family left their farm and headed west on a long journey for California. One of Adam's uncles had actually worked for the Union Pacific Railroad and was present during the pounding of the last golden spike at Promontory Point, Utah, in 1869, so they initially headed north to Nebraska, where they could catch the transcontinental railroad at Omaha and book passage all the way to Sacramento. Adam could then relay stories to his children (as they looked out of the passenger-car windows at the immense prairies awash with herds of sheep, cattle, and buffalo as far as the eye could see), as told him by his own father, of their hardworking, track-laying Uncle Henry and his rather "colorful," well-known exploits that earned him the moniker, "Hell on Wheels," coinciding with the many tent cities popping up as the miracle railroad snaked its way westward. Upon arriving in Sacramento, they made their way to the river dock and caught a ferry bound for San Francisco Bay.

Once in "Frisco," the eight members of the Block family trudged up the gangway onto the rickety transport ship that would take them on the journey south to San Pedro Harbor, Los Angeles. The accommodations they had procured with their diminishing savings secured for them a sardine-like existence for the duration of the voyage, packed as they were in their little forward cabin, tucked deep within the pitching, heaving, leaky bulkhead. The boys loved the occasional bilge rat that scurried by their bunks, but the girls and Emiline were terrified. Famished vermin and their curious nibbling around the feet of his family were the least of Adam's worries. Robbed as he was of even a passing knowledge of the sea by his landlubber life on the farm, he still possessed a keen sense of reading and tracking the weather patterns above his head. This knowledge, or lack thereof, meant life or death on the solid ground of a farm, and Adam was convinced that it was the same life-or-death gamble on the liquid swells now rolling beneath them.

While appreciating his instincts, the Captain, a 19th-century buccaneer, assured Adam that the instability he smelled in the air was common for this time of year and typical of the San Francisco Harbor conditions specifically, and for the Northern California coastline in general. Their southerly transit over 400 miles of Pacific Ocean to San Pedro would be routine.

"He has a deadline to meet, or I'm sure he wouldn't have put out to sea." This, he told Emiline privately, so as not to alarm the children, who were on deck either watching the sailors crawl up and down the rigging like so many spiders or playing with other interesting passengers of younger ages whom, it seemed, were from all parts of the country.

The Captain's rash expediency hearkened back to that fateful, weather-daring decision found in the Bible about which his mother had cautioned Adam on principle, when an Alexandrian corn ship decided to push the nautical boundaries at Fair Havens harbor on the island of Crete and make for better winter anchorage at the Cretan port of Phoenix, just 40 miles to the northwest. That feckless decision set in motion a typhoon of consequences and the fourth and final shipwreck survived by the Apostle Paul.

There was also the poor judgment of King Jehoshaphat, whose newly built ships bound for gold in East Africa were sunk on their maiden voyage right in their hometown harbor of Ezion-geber.

Understandably, Adam did not sleep well that first night. He dreamed that he was back home, salty sweat pouring down his forehead and stinging his eyes as he strained uphill, trying to plow a straight furrow into a shale-blanketed, sun-hardened new field with his horse, Wallace. With a loud *Crack!* the plow had hung up on a large group of igneous rocks in the soil. Wallace reeled and attempted to pull again. But the plow snagged the outcropping once again, pulling up a large, stubborn boulder partially to the surface as Wallace snorted and put his head down, pushing his hooves nearly vertically into the clods of encrusted dirt and clay underneath him. The wood of the plow gave out last-ditch crunching and groaning sounds as Adam attempted to negotiate the steadfast boulder. He gave out a cry of determination from the strain and became aware that his yelp had escaped into the conscious world. He sat up in his bunk and realized with a start that the sound of wood crunching against rock had also leaped from the escapable pages of his imagination onto the inescapable planking of stark reality right underneath his feet!

The rest of his family was up, too, seemingly in the same instant. There were shouts and curses from the sailors above, some so colorful that Emiline would have attempted to cover the virgin ears of her children had not the entire ship violently lurched to starboard, ejecting Maggie and Paul from their berth and sending them rolling onto the rough planking. Fortunately, the others had instinctively hung on to whatever was solid. Emiline bent down to rescue the two from the wet floor—and gasped that it was so. The floor had always been damp and mildewed, but a thin pool of water was now sloshing forward and aft in concert with the upheavals of the ship.

There was a loud *Crack!* like that of a large, weighted tree limb breaking free from its mother trunk, followed by a sickening scraping sound of wood being sheared off and chewed up by teeth from the deep. Then the whole cabin floor pitched and reeled, throwing the entire Block family into a terrified heap against the leaky wall. Water began gurgling up from the widening puddles in the middle of the cabin.

Against a rising river of water pouring down the galley way, Adam tore open the cabin door in an instant. He looked outside, yelling back and forth to a stampede of sailors splashing by about the shape of the ship and quickly pulled in his head, saying as calmly as he could masquerade to his family, "We've run aground. We hit some rocks!" Just then the puddles exploded into geysers of wood splinters and salt water that gushed over their feet as the water level in the cabin began to rapidly ascend up their legs. The children began screaming. Adam and Emiline frantically gathered what belongings were within arm's length, and the eight of them were on the precariously leaning deck in moments.

Amidst howling winds, the Captain was swearing and shouting orders every which way like an illustrious sea warlord when he spied Adam. "Get your family into one of those boats, Mr. Block! Over the gunwale with ya, NOW!" He pointed to one of the lifeboats being lifted over the starboard side. He continued marching aft but turned around and called back to Adam, pointing, "We're off the coast of Santa Cruz! There! Off the port bow!" As if that would bring any comfort to someone who had never set foot in California before and who had seen the Pacific Ocean for the first time only a few days before.

Emiline gathered the shivering, soggy children to herself. She, too, was thinking from her own Bible-rearing childhood that this was just what Paul and Luke must have felt during that first-century disaster, when the prow of their battered boat was violently run aground on a Maltese beach. The exposed stern was instantly broken to bits by the pounding, watery punches of a raging Mediterranean Sea that had unleashed the maritime monster, Euroclydon.

Like Acts, Chapter 27, and to the crew's credit, there was no loss of life, no fresh skeletons added to the growing bone collection down in Davy Jones' locker. The brawny sailors expertly rowed the boats to shore with back-breaking agility as they deftly negotiated their individual skiffs through the treacherously narrow straits. They had to compensate for the fierce tempest moving against them, stirring up waves that juggled them back and forth from certain death on rocks that, if allowed, could have effortlessly shattered the little crafts into tiny bits. Their backs to the shoreline, the passengers in the lifeboats each had a unique view of a stormy horizon that was rising and falling like a teeter-totter, and of the relentless breaking-up of their ship in the receding distance. Within a few harrowing hours, all were safely brought to shore on the rugged coastline of Santa Cruz. The Block family huddled, dripping wet and shivering with cold on the rocky beach, while the Captain walked back and forth, barking salvaging orders to his already-exhausted crew. As he walked by, Adam shook his head in disgust at a man who'd let imprudence overrule warning signs from the heavens, spelling sheer doom for both sailor and farmer.

The family made their way back to Sacramento and caught the Central Pacific Railroad south to Los Angeles. No one in the family wanted to endure another sea voyage.

1887. The first Sunday after arriving in Los Angeles, Adam inquired at the local farmers market about leasing farmland. He received a tip that some excellent land could be obtained some 25 miles to the east in Vista Pacifica, a town that, as Adam would later say, was just "a wide spot in the road" at the time. It wasn't long before Adam had purchased five acres of land in the southwest corner of Vista Pacifica, upon which he built a small, rustic ranch house, a home that would not ever house very many amenities, including plumbing. From here, the family would plant and cultivate both a small walnut and a small peach grove (large, full-grown walnut trees can still be seen in present-day Monument, lining the streets of the neighborhoods built on the original land). Shortly thereafter, Adam leased two separate plots of 20 acres each. One would be used to grow watermelons and the other for cantaloupes, the Southern California soil rich in the prolific nutrients required for these indigenous crops to flourish. "I left the grapes and apricots to the farmers up on the hillside," Adam would say of the soil more conducive for these particular crops that was to be found on the hills east against the San Gabriel mountains.

The small home on the proportionately small plot of land in the center of the leased properties had been built with the last of their money, so the entire family immediately got to work on preparing the soil that would hopefully support their livelihood. Adam hired a few horses and mules from a livery stable in Los Angeles to accommodate the vast agricultural workload now pressing upon the Block family. It was already late in the season, so Adam worked his young brood especially hard for their ages in order to get the land ready for what he hoped would be a bountiful harvest. But the momentum was slowed by Emiline's announcement that she was pregnant once again. Adelaide Block was added in 1889, and the family was now complete.

Adam was respected and well-liked among his friends in the community, and, to his great relief, his farm was prosperous. He was able to purchase the farmland when his leases were expired and expand it every year. By 1895, the acreage had grown tenfold. In spite of all this expansion, Adam never enlarged the little house that he had originally built in 1887.

They all still ate and slept in the same cramped quarters. Adam argued that it kept the children outside and thereby increased their productivity on the farm, and their overall education out in the sunshine. When their last child, Adelaide, was six years old, Adam received his most prodding incentive for adding a room or two to the house: Thirty-seven-year-old Emiline came in one evening and told Adam quite sheepishly that she was going to have *another* baby.

"I thought we was beyond the reproducin' years!" he remarked. To which Emiline just shook her head and looked down at her stomach. Nine months later, on May 20, 1895, a fifth son was added to the Block brood, Colby.

Colby was not as boisterous as his older brothers. Although he had moments of rambunctiousness, he was more sedate overall and allowed his brothers to carry out the more rascally behavior. As the last of eight kids, he was loved and adored by his older sisters, who doted on him like a doll.

Once the excuse of further migration had been put to rest, Emiline was unyielding about her family settling down to attend church each and every Sunday. Adam went along with this, his attitude displaying more shoulder-shrugging resignation than handclapping enthusiasm. Consequently, Colby Block grew up in the church, learning about the mysteries of earthly and heavenly fathers all from the same pew.

As the years wore on, Adam Block seemed to be reverting back to his earlier days of wordlessness. Or, according to Emiline, his words were becoming very, very few—like the drying up of a well. Adam was capable of great, undying love—it was a vast reservoir, deep underground, from which he alone could draw. He was still devoted and reliable, and his disquietude bestowed an aura of stability, and yet it magnified his mystery as well.

Because Emiline's successful attempts at drawing him out were now quite rare, the silence between them was no longer a restful, assured repose. It was a widening, uncomfortable gulf.

By the time Colby was a toddler, Adam not only had very little conversation left in his middle-aged storehouses to share with his fifth son, he was also living elsewhere. His family was told that he had rented the nearby house from an adjacent farmer because their household was simply too crowded. Beginning with Emiline, and as the children grew older, each knew in their own way that the man who was husband and father to them all was living alone to provide himself with necessary isolation and solitude. He still loved them. Deeply. But he was incapable of saying it or showing it by where he lay down his head each night. His love was unconditional. But it needed the protection and insulation his separation provided. They worked the farm together, as that required rigorous labor and not-so-rigorous conversation outside of grunts and groans from the sweat and the strain.

In spite of the mandate from their mother, they grew to look forward to going to the First Christian Church in Vista Pacifica, because their father was also included in her mandate and would be required to sit there with them in the pew, playing referee between them, as he had done for years.

Emiline grew jealous of God. She knew He got more of her cagey husband than she did. It was to His advantage that He was Spirit and not spouse, she groused. Adam was more transparent with someone he could not see, someone who did not have emotional eyes looking back at him. She felt robbed in the stillness—her Heavenly Father cutting in on her dance of faithfulness and obedience with His earthly son.

After so many years of this erosion, one evening Adam's conviction made him linger a little later on the family porch overlooking the majestic mountains beyond the town, and he and Emiline were alone. Adam's presence was now more of an anomaly as he had taken on a night job with the Southern California Land and Water Company, where he oversaw the distribution of water from the Los Angeles river to farmers who paid handsomely for the privilege of having diverted dirt flumes flow with liquid nourishment to their thirsty crops. Emiline did not think the $1.25 he made per night was worth his time away from the family, especially since he had to supply his own horse! (Irrigation was the closest any of them ever came to water, as none of them had learned to swim. Even when the neighbor kids would dam up sections of the river to make a lake to swim in, Emiline refused her frustrated children to participate. After twenty years, the panic of her family's shipwreck off Santa Cruz was evident on their mother during the flood of 1907, when she screamed at them to get to higher ground after it had rained for two straight weeks and the Los Angeles river overflowed its banks and flooded the adjacent farmland with more than two feet of water. She was also the only one allowed to go and draw water from the family well.)

The usual silence on the porch this night (other than the creaking of the two rocking chairs, facing an eastern horizon covered with stars) was suddenly interrupted by a preparatory sigh from Adam followed by an unusual statement,

"I wish you had the *other* husband, Emiline," he said, weighing words as carefully as his flimsy scales would allow.

She looked at him quizzically. He did not return her gaze but kept staring obliquely at the mountains.

"The one I should have been," he continued, strangely innervated.

"I wish I could be more loving, more caring, and, um . . . more talkative. I just can't. I just can't. Somethin' inside me just screams, an' I clam up. My own Pa never gave me any learnin' in talkin', especially to females. An' I have gummed up my relationships with 'em ever since. He didn't give me much education in lovin' neither." His voice was quaking, and Emiline grabbed his scabrous hand. He let her hold it.

"God has been talkin' at me for quite a spell, Emiline." He turned his head. Watery, desperate eyes looking into hers. Unthinkable.

"He's been tellin' me to be a better husband to ya."

Emiline was relieved. At least her Heavenly Father wasn't two-timing her against her husband like she had suspected.

"After all these years . . . you'd think . . . But the *real* me is not very pretty. It's awfully dark down there." He paused, sniffed, and extricated his hand from hers. He was detaching himself, hiding once again that which he felt was hideous and hating the fact that all of this was hurting her.

His head turned, and his eyes once again sought the unfocused comfort of the eastern horizon.

"I just can't," he murmured, clearly rankled by the feeling of helplessness.

"I love you, Adam Block," was Emiline's response to all of this, strongly, passionately, seizing a rare moment. "I love the husband you are and father you are to these here kids, too!"

"I never thought I would let this happen again."

"What happened?" This question was a prompt. Though not inclined to voice it, Emiline would have to admit that this inveterate, duplicitous condition of Adam's was true enough and growing worse as the years wore on. He was wily, in a country-bumpkin sort of way, at dodging and evading certain unsafe conversational subjects of the heart the minute the possibility of personal discomfort and self-revelation loomed.

"Someone has to keep quiet, so's an argument can't fester," he would say.

"What happened?" Emiline repeated.

"My runnin'. Being miles away while I'm standin' right here next to you. Staying where it's safe."

Emiline opened her mouth to speak but thought better of it. Adam continued.

"I don't want my boys to grow up like this. Not knowin' what to say or how to talk to a lady. They should not retreat like their old man. That was drilled into me durin' the War—and we won. But this war is different. It's not only in your guts, uh, your insides, I mean; no, this one's in your spirit, too!

"I don't want to give them this here trait. But, by God, Emiline, I can't help myself." Adam said, his panic presaging future generations. Then the window, like the brief, cloudless light in the eye of a hurricane, started to close once more around Adam's soul, never to be opened again on this Earth.

"You can help yourself, dear!" Emiline grabbed for his hand, but it was unresponsive. Their hands were clasped, but his grip was gone. So, she held on to hope instead.

"You don't have to give it to your sons!" But it was too late. He'd already given it to Colby.

In spite of his dried-up conversation and lack of fatherly energy, Adam Block had a special bond with his youngest son. During the three-month-long harvest season, this was primarily fostered by the four-hour trek by horse-drawn wagon, six nights a week, over the Hollywood Hills, to the two-block-long Los Angeles Public Market on 3rd and Alameda Streets, with a copious wagon load of succulent watermelons or peaches in tow. They would get up at 11:00 p.m. to feed the horses and load the wagon, and start the long journey in the first wee hours of Sunday morning in order to arrive at the Farmers Market by 4 a.m. At such a young age, it was quite a breathtaking sight for young Colby to see the train of wagons snaking their way westward in a long line up the switchbacks of the dirt mountain road, the wagon lanterns swinging on each side, looking like so many candle-holding priests, humming a song of ascents, trekking through the darkness on some lofty vigil.

It was in Los Angeles that Adam would treat his son to a twenty-five-cent breakfast of hot-cakes, which Colby would wolf down, still in plenty of time to rent a stall and sell their melons and peaches at a fair price along with the other costermongers at one of the dozens of other stalls. They always kept a wary eye out for the Russian and Chinese wheeler-dealers, who flocked in like vultures at the end of the day, looking to strike a lucrative deal with any desperate farmer who hadn't yet completely sold his wagon load. After purchasing barley for their horses, father and son would pack up for the return trip home. When Colby wasn't falling into an exhausted sleep on the trip, it afforded father and son time together. Even if a word was not said between them, at the very least, a bond was being formed by their silently sharing the same, bouncing buckboard together. Or walking side by side, leading the tired horses homeward.

At $8.00 a wagon load, the melon and peach sales accounted for a goodly portion of the large family's livelihood. It thereby served as a noble, provisional excuse for the two of them not to be in church that morning. Although they never vocalized this commonality, both Adam and Colby were relieved to have the break from facing God and having to communicate with Him, even though He was easier to talk to than with each other. They both fell under the spell of wishful thinking that the Creator of the universe had His hands full with the folks at the First

Christian Church in Vista Pacifica and could not possibly have the time to be bothered with a bunch of overall-clad farmers hawking their homegrown wares at the makeshift gathering of stalls in downtown Los Angeles.

The First Christian Church of Vista Pacifica was a white-clapboard affair situated on the west end of the township, in the flatlands. Its whole ramshackle construction spoke of a temporary establishment, lying in wait for a more permanent edifice.

It had a white steeple that Colby commented was much too stubby to be supporting something as important as a cross, which was perched on top.

From a very early age, Colby did not go in much for the lengthy sermons provided by the young resident pastor, Phineous Cannon. Pastor Cannon was a very short, pudgy man, "our own little Zacchaeus," the congregation would say, who would use a small, custom-made wooden platform on which to stand behind the pulpit so that the bottom of his chin could barely clear the surface rim. Given his compact spherical dimensions, some would also say that he looked like he had been shot out of his own last name. Even so, he could still fire a sermon with deadly accuracy. Colby would, however, nab just enough information to fire up his own imagination and his pencil. He recognized early on that in order to survive having to sit still under the "Napoleon complex" bellowing from behind the pulpit, an acceptable diversion must be devised. So he regularly stuffed sheets of paper into his faded, hand-me-down (Adam, Jr.-Pete-Paul-Thomas-Colby) Sunday jacket, in order to pass the time. As the youngest, he was farthest down the row in the pew from his parents, so his doodling went undiscovered week after week. One Sunday, Pastor Cannon was preaching a sermon entitled "Trouble in the Treasury Department." He was exploring the twelfth and thirteenth Chapters of the book of John and pondering the question as to why, when each of the disciple's twelve new jobs were handed out by Jesus, did a thief like Judas get to become the keeper of the money bag. Jesus was certainly not hiring according to the ability of the qualified applicants (an equal opportunity employment process Jesus would forever continue, His actions affirming the whole of humanity). Of Judas, he must have known that, three years later, the job would become too much for him. Adam was tapped upon the shoulders by a concerned parent in the pew behind the Block family, who jerked his head to one side indicating the direction requiring Adam's paternal attention. He looked down the row to his left and saw his youngest boy earnestly scribbling away at something. After the service, the paper was seized from the inside pocket of Colby's jacket, and a raw talent was discovered.

Colby Block enjoyed spending his childhood years in Southern California, especially in and around Vista Pacifica. Although his days were filled with back-breaking chores from dawn till dusk that never seemed to be finished, such as milking their three cows, feeding the four horses, two hogs, and a passel of chickens, Colby would always comment for the rest of his life that "hard work never killed anyone." His only break from farm duties was the two-mile walk to the Vista Pacifica Grammar School (that had been built the same year they had arrived in town) where Colby would learn history, math, and phonics English from 8:00 a.m. until 3:00 p.m., along with the ten or twelve other boys and girls on furlough from their own farms. On the regrettably *many* occasions when Colby had to stay after school because of another bout with his natural inclination toward insubordination, he would be forced to run "lickety-split" home to be able to start the evening chores by 3:30, and for his back side to avoid the thick wooden paddle leaning against the corner by the front door of his home.

It was safer for him when he was able to join his mother in the horse and buggy for their weekly trips to Parker's Store to buy groceries for the coming week. The serenity of the excursion was interrupted only once when a group of Mexican *banditos* came riding past them on their way into town. Colby had been warned about them by his father, who had told him to be on the lookout whenever he was on the roads. "Them *banditos*," he would say, "they were up to some no good. They come a-ridin' out of Los Angeles and is always fleein' to the mountains behind Vista Pacifica to hide out for a spell." His mother had grabbed him tightly by the arm, her fingers digging in that she meant business. "Keep your head down, and hush up till they pass, you hear!" Colby could hear the danger in her voice and did as he was told. Almost as soon as it began, the riding thunder diminished, and the dust once again began to settle into the ruts in the dirt road. Both mother and son were still shaken while they made their purchases at the grocery store. They would prefer the flocks of dirty, bleating sheep coming from Los Angeles that occasionally overtook them on their way to market any day over the filthy, caterwauling *pistoleros* who meant nothing but trouble.

Colby had not been provided this much excitement since old lady Ranshaw's barn burned down. He remembered hearing in the night the clanging bells of the horse-drawn water wagon with the members of the Vista Pacifica Volunteer Fire Department clinging, white knuckled, to the rocking sides. He had leapt out of bed and could see the eerie, flickering glow in the distance as the flames rose in the sky.

The wagon had arrived too late, and the barn burned to the ground. After his chores, Colby had ridden his bicycle over to the property the next day to see the smoldering remains, mounds of ashes and bent, scorched iron from which rose trails of white smoke. The area looked like heaps of gray dust that had been randomly swept over steaming, thermal underground hot springs.

One of the favorite stories Colby would later tell his children and grandchildren was the devilish fun he and some of the neighborhood kids would have on Halloween Night. Around the first of October, they would begin collecting wooden sewing spools (more like stealing from their mothers' sewing kits), and carve notches into both of the spool's round edges. On Halloween Night, they would roll up a long piece of string around the spools, and sneak up to windows of unsuspecting neighbors. With clockwork know-how, they would press the spool against a front window, with the string sticking out between their fingers.

With the other free hand, they would grab the string and pull it hard. The spool in the other hand would spin while being held fast against the window, the notches making a tremendous rattling noise that sounded like a Gatling gun going off in the living room of the house. Before the frightened occupants could run to the front door to shake their fists and scream at the little hoodlums, they would instantly weave their way and blend in with other Halloween hooligans, scampering off to the next block of houses, where the joke was repeated on window after window after window. Colby and his gang of Halloween thugs never made their identities known, no matter how official and widespread the neighborhood complaints became, of rattling or soaped windows, and the occasional tipped-over outhouse (or of those that had been stealthily moved back in the night six feet from their original location!).

The delightful terrors of Halloween Night were rivaled only by the colorful tents and beaded doorways of Foxes' Traveling Fiesta Carnival of Mystery that took over the vacant lot at the north end of town every month or so. Palm readers, fortune tellers, seers with crystal balls, fire-breathers, and death-defying acts were all part of the allure for children all over Vista Pacifica, who begged their skeptical parents for pennies to spend at the carnival, promising to first finish their chores before they hoofed it as fast as their little legs could carry them to view the wonders that awaited behind the multitudinous canvases, a Foreign Legion of phantasmagoria.

In addition to his relentless chores on the family farm, Colby endeavored to earn a few extra "pennies" elsewhere. "I was always loadin' something onto wagons or trucks!" he would say later of his odd jobs helping other farmers load gravel for the paving of the local roads, for which his father received $2.00 a day in wagon rent. His work, too, for the wineries in the very vineyards that spread along the foothills of the mountains east of town where he had hunted as a boy was back-breaking, loading the heavy barrels of wine onto trucks bound for the Los Angeles harbor. "Especially since I didn't drink!" he said.

Beginning his tenth year, Colby's summer job was to get up at 5 a.m. in order to get at his task of driving a team of horses that first needed to be harnessed to a hay baler by 6 a.m. so that they could start walking by 7 a.m. in a never-ending circle that gave the machine live horsepower to compress the hay into bales that Colby would then hastily, but with the practiced efficiency of callused hands, wire together. He was given $2.00 a day for work that ended 15 hours later, six times a week.

Colby Block was also a voracious reader. He was constantly being told by his parents to turn out his light and get to sleep because work on the farm would start before sunup. However, the admonition was always presented with a clear view of the boy's nose deep in some book or other. He obtained classic tales from the literary coffers of the schoolmarm, of whom Colby was very fond, at the local Vista Pacifica Grammar School. His mother noticed a running theme in all of the titles, *Oliver Twist*, *Tom Jones*, *Great Expectations*. His favorite was *Ben Hur*, the unlikely novel by his father's old commanding officer, Lew Wallace. Emiline wondered why this penchant for stories about "boys struggling to become men against an overbearing and often cruel system." When asked, Colby either could not or would not articulate any rationale for this pattern and was obviously uncomfortable when confronted. The seeds of his father had definitely found fertile ground and taken root in her youngest boy. Seeds that would spawn the vices of silence. Solitude. Seclusion. She could only hope that his Heavenly Father would get to him first.

God would show himself to young Colby through a miracle. "The miracle of the bicycle and the buck rake," Colby would call it decades later to his children and grandchildren.

Volmer Hackett rode his bike everywhere around town. The steep hillsides in the northeastern portions of Vista Pacifica were easy challenges for Volmer. Even though he was getting on in years, his athletic ability was unseasonable. He was riding home late one moonless night. He had just coasted down the hillside and was going at a good clip when he turned right onto a very dark First Street. It was a familiar route to him, one he had taken hundreds of times before, even at this time of night. As he raced past the machine shop on his right, he did not even see the buck rake that was parked on the street, awaiting repairs. As it was just before harvest time, the owner of the shop was overwhelmed with repair requests and had to park equipment out on the street since there was no more room in his large warehouse. Standing on the pedals, the breeze blowing back his hair, Volmer had momentarily turned to look at a few horses grazing by a fence across the street when the wind was knocked out of him. One of the thick, dark teeth of the buck rake, directly in his path, impaled his tender flesh in an instant. The bicycle slid out from underneath him. The motion of the crash and the weight of his body sent Volmer sliding to the dirt below, during which the blade held fast and ripped a gaping hole in his chest as he fell. Fortunately Volmer's bicycle continued wobbling for a few feet, and eventually crashed into the metal gate of the machine shop, making the first loud noise of the collision. This was heard by Parker Mills, the owner of the shop, who lived next door. He came running out of his house curious as to the origins of the racket. The scene before him was one of shock and horror. He recognized Hackett's bike instantly and then spied the groaning figure in a pool of blood poured out like water, writhing in the street. His chest was laid open, and his beating heart had been dislodged from the cavity and lay next to the body. Trying desperately not to vomit, Parker yelled to his wife Mollie in their house to go and get ole Doc Holland, the beloved physician who would one day be instrumental in building the very first hospital in Vista Pacifica. Ever curious, Parker's wife came over to see what all the panic was about.

It was the blood-curdling scream of Mollie Mills that woke up the Block family, who lived next door, the still, clear night carrying her shrieks over the acreage between them. The entire family was on the scene in moments, still putting on their robes, pants, and shirts. Colby, the fastest runner, was now assigned to get "the Doc." Adrenaline was pumping through his 13-year-old body when Colby banged on the door of the Holland house, yelling Doc's name at the same time.

It took a few minutes for Doc Holland to get his black medical bag and run to the scene. Upon arrival, he squatted down and, in moments, grimly assessed the magnitude of Volmer's condition. It was then that wide-eyed Colby saw him do the unimaginable. He had expected the Doc to send for Pastor Cannon to read Volmer Hackett his last rites. Instead, Doc Holland picked up the beating heart from the street, wiped the dust away, and gingerly placed it back into the victim's heaving, punctured chest. Adam, Pete, and Paul Block helped carry the blood-soaked Volmer Hackett back to the surgical room situated at the rear of the doctor's house. The door was closed for what seemed like hours. Every few minutes, more and more citizens of Vista Pacifica gathered in front of the Holland home as word had passed from house to house of the tragic incident. The swelling crowd included anguished members of

Volmer's family, including Volmer's frantic wife, Trudy, who was ushered out of the cold night air into the Hollands' living room to wait.

Finally, an exhausted Doc Holland appeared on the front porch and immediately thanked those who had been so heroic in helping out. Colby rocked queasily as he noticed that the Doc was still wiping *something* off of his hands! The chill shivered through him as he imagined what it might be! The Doc informed the ensemble that he had repositioned the heart of Volmer Hackett in its proper place and sewed him up as best he could.

"It is now in God's hands," he stated, matter-of-factly. He thanked the crowd again and went back inside his home, closing the front door behind him. Pastor Cannon, who had shown up about halfway through the surgery, called those so inclined to meet at the First Christian Church so that they could set up a 24-hour prayer vigil on behalf of "Brother Hackett." Emiline went to the church as a representative of the Block family.

Colby could not get the gruesome scene out of his mind. It kept playing over and over again, pushing out any other welcome, unrelated thoughts. The only thing that would give him mental respite was to pray as well. So, he did. He did not know Volmer Hackett very well, so he prayed a prayer on behalf of a stranger. All he knew of Mr. Hackett was that he had been the man with his heart lying in the street, on a night Colby would never forget for the rest of his life.

Colby Block would also never forget the outcome.

Volmer Hackett not only lived, but eight weeks later, Volmer Hackett had fully recovered.

Months and even years later, when Colby spotted Mr. Hackett on his new bicycle, he would look up at the sky and nod his head toward the Source of the miracle whizzing by before his very eyes. Colby secretly gave the Great Physician his own dusty heart as well.

The only problem was that Colby himself did the sewing, concealing the personal details of his own miracle from those around him.

At 15, Colby was forced to learn to drive something other than a tractor. He had taken on a delivery job at the local grocery store after school, and the owner had sat him down in his red Studebaker and given the nervous boy a quick lesson. Once he got the hang of it, automobiles of all shapes and sizes would forever catch his fancy.

By 1912, the handsome, 17-year-old Colby Block already had gained quite a reputation for being quiet around the halls and classrooms of the Vista Pacific High School. He was well liked and respected, but his closest friends would have to admit that you had to yank the words out of him. He did not seem shy or intimidated; he just spoke only when there was something he thought important enough to say. He did not waste words. His "yes" was "yes" and his "no" was "no," period—and even they were used most frugally. When something tugged at him enough to form speech, the people around him were all ears. What followed was rare and sure to be important.

He could get away with this around his boyhood friends, who had grown to understand him over the years. But there was one aspect of his life that was not going to honey up so easily to one so attractive yet closed-mouthed as Colby Block. Namely, girls. In the Fall of his junior year, Colby Block gave chase to the cat that had got his tongue all for the sake of the most dazzling girl he had ever seen. Inquiries on the spot produced her name, Doris Wallace, the surname an enchanting and conceivable talisman hearkening back to his father's extraordinary horse (and Civil

War commanding officer!). Her family had arrived in town some months before, and he had first spotted her in history class when his junior year had commenced that September. It took some weeks for him to progress from beyond open-mouthed gawking, whether in the classroom, in the hallway, or outside at lunch, to actually saying "Hello." As a matter of fact, their first meeting had to be arranged by his best friend who . . . had another friend . . . who knew a friend . . . of Doris's best friend who . . . could gently let Doris know that there was this boy who . . . It was good news indeed that traveled back to Colby through this far-flung chain of accomplices: Doris Wallace was in recovery, repairing from a recent summer fling, and was not yet "spoken for."

Colby, shuffling his feet with his hands in his front pockets, had stammered out something about the weather without ever so much as looking her straight in the eye. She looked at him pitifully. But there was something charming about this good-looking boy that intrigued her. Colby would say later that the second greatest miracle, right below the one about Volmer Hackett's heart, would be when Doris Wallace actually went out on a date with him after his pathetic attempt at conversation during their first introduction. It was on October 9, 1912. Colby would remember the date forever because he fretted and prepared for the date *forever*.

It was a school dance, so the entire student body of Vista Pacifica High School was aware of the pair: Native-born Colby Block and the fresh-off-the-train-from-Montana Doris Wallace. After proving time and time again that his feet were both left, and spilling apple cider on his hand-me-down (Adam, Jr.-Pete-Paul-Thomas-Colby) jacket, he had walked her home on an unseasonably balmy night. As it seemed to always be the harvest season, his father had warned him not to stay out too late, as there was early work pressing on the morrow. So, they only talked briefly out in front of Doris's home (complete with parental porch-spying by Mrs. Wallace from a darkened front window). But all this had transfixed Colby Block into a silent swoon, which Doris Wallace enjoyed delicately fanning over the next few weeks.

Colby's fire was quenched abruptly. Almost as soon as it began.

He appeared to be backing off from his pursuit of Doris Wallace. Inexplicably. He remained cordial to the fair and beautiful object of his first serious crush, but it seemed to Doris that the stiff pleasantries were a harsh turn of events from the awkward, flowery speeches delivered with perspiring terror by Colby just the week before. She could never divine what had actually happened, although, with some relief she did finally drag out of Colby that the change in him had nothing to do with *her*. But it still hurt, and it seemed to her that, by his own doing, he would never give himself the chance to see the walls of privacy that he was erecting before they reached heights too high for either side to scale.

As heartbreaking as this transformation had been, Doris was now once again available, and it was not long before another suitor sought her company. But by the time another boy did show up, Doris's warming to him was diffident, and the prospects of their dating were slow-going and very tentative, as her experience with men up to that time had now resulted in two bitter disappointments in succession.

After graduating from High School, Colby worked for the Union Oil Company in nearby Burbank. His small frame gave him the unenviable task of actually climbing up into the oil tanks to check their levels, during which time he kept his nose sniffing the airwaves for news of the turmoil on the world scene and the rumblings of possible war in Europe. He began to collect newspaper clippings from at home and abroad as events unfolded. When the *Lusitania* was torpedoed and sunk by a German U-boat in May of 1915 (his parents had told him in great detail about the horrors of being in a shipwreck, and Colby could only imagine this scene, where more than 1,300 people died), it looked to Colby as if the rough-and-tumble United States of America was eventually going to lend a hand and get involved. This meant that that dire branch of the federal government, the Selective Service, would begin plucking eligible soldiers out of its continental ranks, including 20-year-old farm boys from Vista Pacifica. Later he obtained another clipping from overseas (that had to be translated) which was an analysis, four months after the fact, of chemical warfare, specifically the impact of poison chlorine gas which was used on an Algerian unit of the French army during the 2nd Battle of Ypres. It was clear to Colby that things were tensing up, so he had enlisted in the U.S. Army before Uncle Sam could have the imperious opportunity to tap him on the shoulder and say, "I want you!" He was "chomping at the bit" he would later say, describing himself rather than "champing" horses about which the phrase originated. He wanted to "to get out there and defend my country against its enemies."

After surviving the demeaning tortures of boot camp, Colby was assigned to a platoon of soldiers stationed at Fort Ord in Monterey, California, awaiting a call to go overseas. Colby liked the military. It suited him. He toyed with the idea of making the armed forces a career, for he discovered to his joy that it was one of the few places where one could succeed going up the chain of command saying sentences, like the haircuts, that are short, clipped, and cropped. No further questions.

Idleness, in all mankind, is a troublesome business. When entertained too long, it grows like a shadow, darkening perspectives as it tends to make people become too ingrown for their own good. In just such a complacent environment were the secrets of Colby's heart challenged.

A tall, very smart, mountain-of-a-man with a blond crew-cut and piercing blue eyes (with the beginnings of a stellar collection of military honors strewn like a clothesline across his jacket) named Lieutenant Lewis, sought brusquely to rip the stitches out of then-Sergeant Block's chest in order to examine his heart. The test was not along the stiff lines of his ability to lead a squad of buck privates, follow orders, march in step, handle a rifle, or finish an impossible obstacle course. No, the test was directed at his faith. Lieutenant Lewis wore proudly his "colors," which were not only his ever-growing regiment of ribbons, stacks of chevrons on sewn patches, and gleaming medals (with still enough room for the coveted and soon-to-be-awarded Purple Heart), he also despised those who gave the slightest inclination that they believed in God, and made it his personal, vindictive crusade to efficiently trim this sort of fat from his platoon.

There were three of them this time. Miller, Swanson, and Block.

There seemed to be an extra measure of scrutiny and even cruelty applied to them as soon as it was leaked that they were "believers." Longer night shifts, harder workouts, more frequent latrine duties. The three Christians swallowed hard at this singling out. There was no justice in the hierarchy. No one would believe the likes of these whining Jesus boys against the acclaimed Lieutenant Lewis. They suffered in silence . . . a fate which greatly agitated Miller and Swanson, but which was very agreeable to Block.

Except for one particular day when Colby's silence did not protect him. He was cornered in the Mess Hall by Lieutenant Lewis and a few of his fellow atheist lieutenants. Over the years, Lieutenant Lewis had obtained enough knowledge to make him dangerous, and he went a-hunting for Sergeant Block, looking to pick a fight.

"Hey, Block!" Lieutenant Lewis pushed him hard in the back, spilling his tray of food. Colby spun around, stiff at attention before he even stopped spinning. He saluted.

"Sir!" he yelled. Head high. Back straight. Lieutenant Lewis got right in his face.

"Sergeant, I hear your loving God had it in for, what's his name?" he asked rhetorically with mock curiosity. "Ah, yes, Esau!" he continued, with a satisfied, malignant smile. "From the very beginning, the poor sap never had a fighting chance!" he sneered.

Colby stood petrified, unable to move and unclear of just how he should respond, if at all. If there was any space between their noses, Lieutenant Lewis closed the gap tightly and yelled in Sergeant Block's face,

"YOUR GOD HATED THAT BOY BEFORE HE WAS EVER BORN! YOUR GOD IS NOT LOVE, YOUR GOD IS A FILTHY HYPOCRITE!"

He stared at Colby, giving him a look that dared him to reply. He slowly backed his face away and looked at his fellow lieutenants, who were smirking with satisfaction.

Right or wrong, Colby saw this as an invitation to speak and desperately tried to cull something intelligent from his churchgoin' past.

64

"God . . . chose . . . another, sir." He stammered just under his breath.

"WHAT WAS THAT, SERGEANT?"

"He chose Jacob, to be the father of a . . . nation . . . sir."

"REALLY?" Lewis smiled wickedly while his fellow lieutenants continued looking on smugly. Just then Colby noticed that this particular corner of the Mess Hall had gone deathly still. Everyone was watching the one-sided shouting match with furtive glances disguising their great anticipation and even fear for the outcome. Lieutenant Lewis was screaming once again,

"THE ONE YOUR GOD HATED WENT AND STARTED HIS OWN EDOMITE ARMY, AND THEY WERE AT WAR WITH YOUR LITTLE JEWISH NATION FOR THOUSANDS OF YEARS! YOUR GOD IS A PATHETIC TROUBLEMAKER, AND YOU'RE A FOOL TO BELIEVE IN HIM!"

"Its . . . election . . . sir."

"WHAT? SPEAK UP, SERGEANT!"

"Election. God chose to make the two nations, sir."

"Really?" Lieutenant Lewis's smile was lethal.

Colby sucked in his breath and spoke as authoritatively as his trembling body would allow,

"He is sovereign, sir. He can . . . do . . . what . . . He . . . pleases . . . sir!"

Lieutenant Lewis was back in Colby's face again, mocking and hissing at once,

"Like convincing little know-nothing punks like you that He loves you while He goes around hating and damning anyone else He . . . what did you say, *elects*?"

Sergeant Colby Block barely nodded.

"You and your priggish, pitiful religion make me sick, Sergeant!" He pulled away, nodding to his compatriots. But before they walked out of the Mess Hall, he turned around, glared at Colby, and jeered, "Sycophant!"

Standing there, Colby was dumbstruck—not only at the unprovoked dressing down by his superior officer but also at an insulting-sounding word he had never heard before. It was right then and there that Colby Block decided he would imitate the God of the Bible in the same way as the Lieutenant's accusation. He, too, would hate who he hated and love who he loved. Topping the list in the former category was Lieutenant Brunswick Lewis. But before this newfound resolution could be further antagonized by Lieutenant Lewis (and Sergeant Block face a highly likely court-martial when eventually, from a loss of words, he might surely punch the Lieutenant squarely on his arrogantly jutting jaw), the United States of America was mobilized to participate in the First World War to expunge the Germans from Allied backyards, and Sergeant Block was safely transferred, first to England and then to France, in 1919.

The dangerous period of idleness had ended.

A year later, Colby Block returned to Vista Pacifica, honorably discharged and his aspiring career in the military coming to a screeching halt. No one knew why this change came about. It was rumored that something significant must have happened during his active tour of duty in the French countryside. When courageously broaching the subject back home, all anyone could get out of Colby was a faraway look, a regretful sigh, and the comment expressed with finality, "There are no atheists in foxholes!" It was there that the conversation would end. Along with Colby Block, there were six others from Vista Pacifica who were coincidentally in Company C, and none would shed any more light on their overseas experiences.

Colby Block did not recognize Vista Pacifica when he returned home from the Army. The main street up the hillside was now completely lined with thriving new businesses, or enlargements of old ones, busy merchants bustling about the grocery store, bicycle shop, drugstore soda fountain, feed and fuel store, real estate office, bank, post office. Housing had exploded and expanded all over the hospitable areas of the mountainside. Horses were slowly being put out to pasture as more and more automobiles noisily made their way around town, which meant that the new livery stable was hanging onto its reins for dear life against replacement by this new mode of transportation.

In spite of this wave of the future—compliments of Henry Ford—"The Funicular" cable-car system still slinked its way non-stop up and down the township's most popular incline, although it was no longer pulled by mule—it was now powered electrically. This was a fortunate advancement, as the mule had refused to pull the car any longer. Up to this time, the mule's job had been only to pull the car uphill. He was carted behind the passengers on a coupled flat bed for the return trip to the bottom of the hill. On a particular day, however, the brakes had given out on the downward route and the cable car, with terrorized mule in tow, went careening and screeching down the boulevard, skipping the tracks and tipping over at the bottom of the hill, pitching its two-and-four-legged passengers helter-skelter as it finally slid to a stop, fortunately just before slamming into the pumps of the Chevron Gas Station directly in its path.

The mule gave notice immediately.

The street had been widened again since Colby had been gone, and "The Funicular's" main purpose these days seemed to be to carry more and more prospective buyers to view properties higher and higher up the hillside.

The town is putting on a whole new face, he was thinking. But there was another new face in town that turned his head faster than any growth spurt in Vista Pacifica, namely Melba Moore.

The Moores had arrived in Vista Pacifica in 1920 from Long Beach. They had come to California from a farm in eastern Kansas (later, Melba would wistfully tell her grandchildren stories of her watching the latest contraption of Orville and Wilbur Wright fly wildly overhead and out-of-state when she was a little girl on the farm). Melba's brother-in-law was a builder. While working for a contracting firm in Long Beach, he took a bus tour that had been attractively arranged by the Vista Pacifica Real Estate Office in order to witness firsthand the building boom going on in and around Hollywood, and to make their own personal bids for available property before it was snatched up by others. Shortly thereafter, the brother-in-law convinced the entire family to move north.

While her husband built, Melba's sister managed the Pacifica Palace Hotel, a spectacular structure boasting more cupolas per square foot than any other hotel in the area. It was built in 1888 and was considered the sister hotel to the great Santa Rosa Hotel in nearby Burbank. They engaged in a healthy rivalry over the next 50 years, as there were plenty of guests for each. Both boasted grand ballrooms in which the very best in full-orchestra dance music was offered. Ironically, both hotels fell into disrepair around the same time and were torn down to make way for new post offices within the same year, 1938.

"You know what they say, neither sleet, nor snow, nor grand hotels would stop the mail," Melba would say later of her sister's "baby."

Colby Block and Melba Moore had their first date at the very first civic dance he ever attended, held in the Grand Ballroom of the Pacifica Palace Hotel. After his discharge from the Army, he had gone to work (via bicycle) in the local drugstore soda fountain where he had met fellow soda jerk Melba. Colby prided himself on making the most delicious chocolate malts anywhere. "The secret's in the ice cream," he would tell salivating grandchildren decades later. "Always load a few scoops of vanilla ice cream into the glass first, like ice, and then pour the chocolate malt over it. And don't forget to use *real* malt powder—that's the secret!"

In addition to the chores that still called his name on the family farm, the drugstore hours were long and hard, so a Saturday night social in town was a welcome change of pace from a lifestyle that offered very little time, or money, for recreation. It was also a welcome relief for hundreds of couples, able to two-step and waltz with the best of them, from all parts of the San Fernando Valley, who would hop in their "horse 'n buggies" or Model-Ts, and go to wherever the latest dance was being held.

The plucky Melba was shorter than Colby. With even shorter brown hair, and a matching set of deep, brown eyes, she had a sturdiness that attracted him. She, too, was enamored by this handsome, 22-year-old local boy. It was because of his family name (now deeply rooted in the town's historic origins) that the romance between favored-son-eligible-bachelor Colby Block and sweet-pretty-and-sturdy Melba Moore became city-wide news in a matter of days.

In spite of Colby's strong desire to have a quiet wedding, consisting of just a few close family and friends (which, considering the size of his own, would itself be a noteworthy crowd), their marriage in 1923 was a grand event in the life of the town that was not to be missed by anyone.

The wedding was held at the First Christian Church, and the building was filled with more souls than had darkened its doors in years. The congregation over the past decade had been shrinking, much to the hapless embarrassment of Pastor Phineous Cannon, who also presided sentimentally over the Block-Moore ceremony. Of Pastor Cannon and the wedding, all Colby would say was that "He tied the knot, and he tied it pretty tight, too!"

More recently, the church numbers had significantly dwindled, which made the Building and Loan Company next door to the church lick its chops in hopes that the hallowed house of God would eventually fold. This declivity was icily excused by Pastor Cannon, God's ombudsman, as the victimization of corruption from Hollywood.

"The culture is changing!" he would say, with end-of-the-world urgency.

"The people are still coming out and sitting in rows week after week, but they're in theater seats now, not pews! They have swapped the pulpit for the big screen. They have exchanged the preacher for their favorite movie star. They now prefer a love story or some swashbuckling adventure set in some exotic location over a good story from the Bible!"

There was truth to this, and the numbers bore this out. Eventually, the darkened movie house, with its silver screen, won out over the enlightened house of God, with its Savior. Literally. Colby and Melba Block remained steadfast members until the day the church finally had to close its doors. Forcibly retired, Phineous Cannon was stricken but not surprised when his prophecy came true, and he received the news that the First Christian Church was to be torn down to make way for a new movie house. Vista Pacifica already had their Palace Theatre, but the glut of motion pictures being churned out by the dream factory to the west demanded more venues in which to screen them. People flocked to the choices provided by both.

Even without a church in town, Colby and Melba Block stayed committed to working with their hands and walking humbly with their God. Living quietly and minding their own affairs, however, was another matter entirely; Melba made this discrepancy more known around town than Colby. When asked about his spirituality by other displaced former members of the First Christian Church, Melba would say of her very private husband,

"You know, I think his life verse is Proverbs 3:32, where it says, 'His secret is with the righteous.' Only problem is Colby *keeps* it that way!"

In hopes that proximity would stoke the fires of their communication, Melba quit her job at the drugstore, and Colby left his next job, as a salesman for the Standard Oil Company (a company that achieved the impossible by turning Colby Block into a crack salesman), and the two of them started an insurance agency together, which had its official birth with the State of California on April 7, 1927. Capitalizing on their vision that the influx of the "horseless carriage" was permanent, they began selling auto-insurance policies at 25 cents apiece door to door in the neighborhoods of Vista Pacifica. They worked out of their home at first (they would not move into an "official" office building until 1946), with Colby acting as front sales-man and Melba answering the phone with the self-proclaimed title of "Secretary Treasurer." From the very first policy sold to Mrs. Tanby, their diligent enterprise would be rewarded by a long-standing family business that would serve the community for generations, particularly because Colby Block was not only viewed as a man of keen business acumen but also lionized as one of sterling integrity who could be fully trusted and reliable in any situation at a mere giving of his word—his bond.

And Colby Block would not have his reputation sullied.

It was about this time that Colby purchased his own first automobile, a Model-T Ford for a whopping $500.00—the total sum of which was completely borrowed from the Vista Pacifica Bank. This afforded the couple mobility (most of the town was now fully paved—except for some roads at the top of the hill, where the town of Vista Pacifica had not yet crept—and was filling up with Ford touring cars!) that allowed them to go on their favorite Sunday afternoon "date"—watching the open-cockpit airplanes take off and land at the nearby United Airport, an aeronautical pastime Colby had secretly tried only once as a passenger while escaping the watchful radar of his protective wife.

By 1924, rumors began swirling that some architect from Hollywood had bought a good portion of the mountain behind Vista Pacifica and was going to carve a movie star's face into the cliff. This was an urgent rallying cry for the remnant of the First Christian Church, who got together one night at the Block's home to discuss this dilemma of the Hollywood influence and the sad fact that there was no church in town to stem its evil tide.

Among those in the group was Roy Mueller. He was a realtor in town and proposed the idea of buying an available piece of property at the base of the mountain on a dirt road, recently named Ridgeway Avenue, that commanded an astounding view of the Pacific Ocean. Citing unpredicted financial complications, a previous commercial venture had suddenly fallen out of escrow, and the property was now once again up for grabs. But they had to act quickly, as it would not be available for long in a rapidly growing town such as theirs. And act quickly they did. It was the quickest business decision ever made in church history. The little band of survivors rising from the ashes of the First Christian Church, now the Orpheus Theatre, pooled their resources together and purchased the property offered privately by Roy Mueller before a more public auction would have a chance to bid the property out of their financial means.

They met sedulously every week—a real, New Testament house church. Only their agenda was not stamping out the legalism of the Pharisees or running from the clutches of Caligula. No. *This* house church was engaged in conceptual discussions ranging in everything from the cost of construction, to the style of architecture, to who would be the pastor, to what they were going to name the new church in the first place.

"'First Christian Church,' of course," said Hazel March. "After all, that's where we've all come from."

"It should be a different name. 'First Christian Church' gives memories of a dead church with hardly any people in it," responded Roy Mueller to the nodding of heads in approbation.

"It was only that way because of those sinful movies!" Hazel had hit it on the head. This opinion was unanimous. National Prohibition was leaking like a sieve and now, in further degeneration, scantily clad starlets were cavorting about on film nightly at two standing-room-only locations—speakeasies with ushers—right here in downtown Vista Pacifica!

"This town's like a bunch of wayward children who need a good whoopin' from their father!"

"*That* should be the name then!" said Earl Sweitzer.

Colby Block raised his hand and said, "But we need to reach this community as well." No one could argue with one so respected in the community, particularly with upstart Hollywood breathing down their necks. Truly, their neighbors' only hope was salvation by grace.

"It should be about evangelizing, then."

After a few more minutes of discussion that quickly turned into hours and days, the puzzle pieces were satisfactorily fitted together and a name unanimously approved by all: Our Father's Evangelical Church.

"Should we join up with a denomination?" asked Roy Mueller.

"No," responded Colby, flatly, before the echo of Roy's question had subsided.

"I'm not going to have any blood on my hands from hacking up the body of Christ into separate parts, all wrapped up in butcher paper so to speak, just so's they can be sold off to picky customers with preferred tastes in rumps, breasts, thighs, and drumsticks!"

The rest of the group all laughed at this audacious word picture, but the point beneath made them squirm slightly.

"OK, non-denominational," was the quick consensus. "Now what's the church going to look like?" asked Melba.

"Big steeple. Nothin' stubby," said Colby, thinking back on his impression upon first sight of the First Christian Church. "An' a cross high up so everyone can see who really paid for the place!" Everyone chuckled respectfully at this profundity.

"It should be colonial, like our founding fathers," said Earl Sweitzer, American History Buff.

"No. Gothic. To match the Old World architecture of the town," said Roy Mueller, Realtor.

Conforming to real estate won out over repeating history. "And brick—for permanence in the community," Colby added.

The only connection to their past would be the rehiring of Phineous Cannon as the Senior Pastor, as much due to sentiment as compassion against his fading abilities.

Weeks turned into months of often heated, detailed planning. Every adornment, flourish, and clerical blandishment was given a detailed examination of comparing-and-contrasting exactitude. From the dimensions of the baptistery, to the placement of the pews; from the depictions in the stained-glass windows, to the number of burnished florets on the bronze candelabras; from the tapestry hanging in the narthex, to the verse engraved on the communion table. "Where is Bezalel and Oholiab when we need them?" queried a frazzled Charles Pendleton. His reference was to that multi-talented twosome of Old Testament craftsmanship, who were commissioned to have their designing hands over every creative cubit of God's new traveling tabernacle.

Donations flooded in. Finally, after nearly a year of labor pains, Our Father's Evangelical Church was finally born in the hearts and minds of the house-church membership.

By 1926, construction was underway.

Right underneath the gigantic chin of the movie star!

By the time the church was finally dedicated in 1930, the carving of the movie star's face had been scrapped, and Vista Pacifica, like biblical Abram, Sarai, Simon, Levi, and Saul, had received a brand-new name, which meant that the local businesses in town would surely follow. The first to change was the Pacifica Palace, which became the Monument Grand Hotel.

The locals all agreed that God must be on the side of the new church, as its building progress was not hindered even by the stock market crash of 1929 nor impeded by the Great Depression that ensued. As a matter of fact, the project gave more job opportunities to those who needed them, and even more still volunteered their efforts for a cause they felt was greater than themselves and the current economic plight of the country as a whole.

By this time, the Blocks had a one-year-old toddling around their home. Even though Colby had come from a household of eight children, the adjustment to Seth Block dramatically changed their peaceful home. His antics were all boy. The noise increased. The list of broken heirlooms lengthened. The patience of parents was tested. And the opinion of both parents was unanimous.

They would have only one of these.

But the growing pains associated with raising Seth Block were nothing compared to the growing pains of Our Father's Evangelical Church.

The first Sunday started out well enough. The main sanctuary was jammed with the displaced membership of the First Christian Church, others desirous of finding a new church home, and citizens curious about the only church in "Monument," as well as civic dignitaries.

It was a grand affair.

Pastor Cannon was magnificent, and youthful. Getting behind the pulpit once again (with the aid of his little booster platform) seemed to have trimmed 20 years off his life and given him back the exuberance of his prime. Now that a voice had been given to his long-time neighbor and foe, Hollywood—its movies now had sound—he was very anxious to get back in the fray of spiritual warfare and use his oratory calling with aplomb to counter the culture and provide well-needed living water and bread of life to those who only knew how to slurp soda and munch on popcorn while watching the "talkies."

A Deacon Board was selected: Farley Dobbs, Earl Sweitzer, Charles Pendleton, Morgan Pierce, Roy Mueller, Franklin Mullens, Noel Saunders, Wyatt Dupont, and Colby Block. At their first meeting, Wyatt Dupont was nominated as Chairman of the Board, with Noel Saunders as Secretary. With its pulpit filled and its leadership in place, Our Father's Evangelical

Church, the only church in Monument, California, was ready to take in customers.

The first sign of controversy started out as just a suspicion. Colby came home after his monthly deacon meeting and would offer Melba very little information under the guise that he was committed to the strictest of confidentiality, which excluded the wives of all Board members. (This successful, closed-mouth unity was quite unique to this period in the church's brief history. Stories abounded later where issues requiring the utmost in "confidentiality"—when dedicated deacons had taken a blood oath forming a pact of secrecy, "What is about to be said in this room, stays in this room!"—around some highly explosive, controversial information that needed to be handled with the utmost delicacy, timing, and church discipline. Yet it still mysteriously poured out as through a sand sifter, only to find the very next day a blushing wife of one of the deacons hearing every titillating detail of the whole story verbatim from the unsaved third checker at the local grocery store! With this example from their leadership, it was no wonder that sometimes the family of God could process and disseminate private news faster and more efficiently than *The Daily Granite*. A danger that a later O.F.E. Pastor Angus Ritchie would counter with the battle cry, "I'll take ten child molesters over one gossip in the church!"). Colby did say one night, however, that he thought Morgan Pierce was "as slippery as an eel," and he would have to keep his eye on him.

This could be lightly shrugged off in comparison to the stupendous first year the church was having in all of its ministries.

But in February 1931, Phineous Cannon fell gravely ill and died within a week. Now the nine-member Board was, for the first time, flung headlong into a search for a new Senior Pastor.

Franklin Mullins had some speaking skills and occupied the pulpit as best he could. But even in his old age and small stature, Phineous Cannon had left some very large shoes to fill, indeed (either on or off the booster stool behind the pulpit).

What with the wiggle room inherited from his predecessor's footprints, Franklin did his own brand of fancy footwork. He had a knack for slipping in a weekly warning for the octet of his newly installed fellow deacons dispersed among the congregation. They were to stand firm and stay that way, sober-minded about the enormity of their calling and single-minded about their moral responsibilities.

"Just a few short months after his Jerusalem arrival, prestigious priest Ezra was busy trying to make the Temple sequel sincere. No sooner had he started praying a foundation, when up confessed some of his top-notch field hands, including unfaithful church leaders! The ministry miscreants had 'led the way,' indulging in some very poor lifestyle choices—namely intermarrying and procreating with foreign women—ignoring the biblical fact that 'iron does not mix with clay!' Ezra had a cultic conniption fit, to which God said of the nuptial neighbors, 'Put them away!'

"For the same loose living, a cursing Nehemiah beat some of the men and pulled out their hair!

"Two months later, every last one of the aliens had been shown the Temple door. Come rain or shine, all should plainly read and obey the 'No Trespassing' sign hung over their own personal, pagan territories—especially our leaders!"

Much to Mullins' sermonizing surprise, his "sign" theme would soon gain traction.

During this season, when no one was present, Colby would spend countless, restorative hours in the main sanctuary of the church, alone. Here he felt he could talk to God best, standing on the promises in the gap of the empty pews.

His strength was in his solitude.

Weeks and months wore on with nary a pastor in view. The church languished in idleness. Colby Block had seen this stagnation scenario play out before in the Army and was fearful that the congregation and the Deacon Board would turn in on itself.

In an effort to head off this possibility, Colby suggested that the Board take down the signs above the exit doors in the main sanctuary that said, "You are now entering the mission field."

"Why don't we stop fretting about our own problems and bring the lost *inside* the church, in droves? Then we can change the signs to read, 'You are now *exiting* the mission field!'" Colby said, somewhat facetiously.

"That should not be, Block. We should not be confined to a building. Wherever we go in this community, across the country, or, even around the world, for that matter, there goes the church! It's us, after all. The church is us!" said Earl Sweitzer, missing Colby's point entirely.

Nevertheless, the earlier concept was met with vicious objections and an intensity that far outweighed the importance of the issue. After all, they were just signs. But they had been a "tradition" as far back as the First Christian Church. So, tempers flared, and voices were raised. It was all for the sake of having an argument, no matter how specious. At least the grousing and complaining was something to do to pass the time while they waited for a new pastor to show up, roll up his sleeves, and referee. It was a clear sign to Colby Block that idleness had come to roost and had taken root, sending out shoots deep into the very seats in which they now sat.

This was not the only trouble with signage. As the congregation began to believe that a new pastor was not even a distant speck on the horizon, a member of the church with a penchant for the apocalyptic began plastering signs around the church saying, "Pray for Revival!" Colby wasted no time tearing these down the minute they were taped to the various walls and doors around the church campus, calling them a "desperate attempt to incite a spiritual riot! It won't be the real thing, I can assure you!" He told Melba in a rare, prolonged conversation, "If we ever needed a real revival, it will be like the Second Coming in the book of Matthew, obvious to everyone. You know, like lightning coming out of the sky from east to west. That engine will not be cranked by a few pathetic signs. I don't much go in for that romantic, German poet, Novalis, when he said, 'It is certain my conviction gains infinitely the moment another soul will believe in it.' What a character! No, these here signs are just asking for a hoax."

Where did that come from? thought Melba, always having to remind herself of Colby's voracious appetite for reading that had begun at a very early age. Compact quotes from Plato, Aristotle, Tertullian, and Augustine could pop up at any moment and surprise anyone within earshot.

Even though an early-riser from his boyhood farming days, Colby never had any "devotions" in the morning like normal church-goin' folks. When Melba asked him about this peculiar behavior in the beginning stages of their marriage, he had quoted Sophocles at her, "One has to wait until evening in order to see the splendor of the day," and the subject was closed.

As with so many of these kinds of conversations, Melba knew that there was so much more to her husband than she was getting. So much more going on beneath the surface, where no one was allowed to plumb the secret depths. Once again, the shade had been pulled down over Colby's soul, and the brief period of illumination that always teased her ended. "MEN!" she said to herself as she thought of the often lonely, gutless preoccupations of the male species. "They live in a world all their own!"

"I'm sure he'll go and shut himself up in the bedroom again this evening. Or run down to the church to sit in the empty sanctuary!" she mused aloud, noticing that the tone in her voice was laced with a jealousy of Colby's God, who seemed to have captured the lion's share of her husband's communication. She knew Colby loved her, deeply. He was devoted and loyal to his core, till death do they part. But his expectations for himself were always a high-jump bar set at a neck-craning height, far above the reflection in the mirror and its behavior on the street, or in their marriage. A large compartment of his life would always be under lock and key, and it seemed that only God himself would ever know the combination.

What was Colby really thinking? Would he ever come out of hiding? What did he fear?

He was her rock, but she was never allowed to pick it up and look at what might be squirming underneath. For whatever reason, there was a terrified little boy in the heart of every man, even those with the strongest of exteriors.

Colby reserved his tears for big-ticket tragedies: When each of his parents died, when his older brother Thomas was hit and killed by an automobile, and when the family farm was finally sold off and their old ranch house burned down to make room for the short-lived municipal airport.

"What's wrong, Honey? What's eatin' you?" Melba felt like she'd asked this question a hundred times in their marriage.

"It's nothing, Honey. I'm fine," was Colby's answer, also given a hundred times in their marriage.

She knew that, occasionally, Colby confessed what was going on in his life to his friend Cyril Holbert, a "safe" male who never edged his way in too close. So, Colby had it in him. The question was how much of "it" would he give to her just now.

"Colby, I know you. You are preoccupied. Is it the church?"

"No. I'm fine!" he answered, terse and disconsolate.

Melba knew the signals. Colby was not going to open up. As they looked on from the hereafter, the closed lips down the previous line of Block men cracked ever-so-slightly into a proud smile as the DNA of manufactured independence that required minimal communication hopped, skipped, and jumped in perpetuity out of the generational gene pool.

There was a *Crash!* from the kitchen that took a relieved Melba out of her hopeless reverie. Seth was at it again . . .

Finally, a new pastor was found, Wesley Zimmerman. The congregation was elated at the news, and the night he was voted in was quite the celebration. Melba thought that this closure would help ease the preoccupations of Deacon Block. But, for some inexplicable reason, it only deepened them. Now the Deacon Board would meet frequently to hammer out the details of the coming new pastor. It seemed to Melba that these meetings would now be exciting, or even mundane, when weighed against the previous month's silly sign scrimmages. They should be anything but controversial.

One particular Deacon meeting lasted well past midnight. Upon coming home, Colby stormed into the living room, red-faced. He walked right past Melba and slammed the door to their bedroom behind him.

Panting, he reached under his side of their bed and slid out a metal-edged chest of blue corduroy, from which he extracted his secret journal that he had started when he was 17 years old.

He took a pen from the desk and began writing.

May 13, 1933
Lord, please forgive me, but I need to leave this church . . .

INTERLUDE

"Sycophants! If I hear one more time 'That's how we have always done it,' heads are gonna roll!' That's what I had first heard he said."

"What is a 'sycophant' anyway?"

It was "Guys Night Out." I was sitting at a dark-green booth surrounded by lush ferns of the same color in a very trendy, upscale restaurant in Burbank that had served the movie-making establishment for more than sixty years. We actually saw Charlton and Lydia Heston among a large crowd of people at a long table in the back, and Diane Keaton chatting with another lady in the bar area. This place was always good grazing ground for celebrities. Opposite me were Tristan Holbert and, a pleasant surprise, Terry Cronklin (grandson of my surly childhood substitute Sunday school teacher, the sourpuss Virgil Cronklin), who was in town on business in Los Angeles, from where he makes his permanent home in North Carolina. All three of us were famished from busy days that had neglected lunch.

Second only to the virgin birth, it was nothing short of a miracle that the three of us had been able to carve out any hours during the peak crunch time of a very hectic Christmas season, let alone that our gracious wives had agreed to our need for some convivial male bonding during such an inopportune time.

At middle age, Terry was already looking like a gourd in the making, with faint wrinkles calling to one another in a unified effort to organize a search party and fan out from his large, bulbous nose. I shuddered when I first saw him in the restaurant lobby. He was looking so much like his grandfather.

"It's someone who, uh, underhandedly, tries to please someone. You know, get on their good side, no matter what the cost. To curry favors. Usually they have some ulterior motive, a swindler of sorts. Unctuous, smarmy," was the best I could explain my grandfather's favorite noun to Terry.

"You mean a flatterer?—like Iago from *Othello*?" asked Terry.

"Yeah, he would be a good example, I think," I said.

"That's what happened, all right!" said Tristan smugly, completely uninterested in our wordsmithing at the moment. "My father told me the whole story that he got straight from his father!" "Your grandfather wasn't even there!" I countered, coming right back from our digression to the argument at hand.

"At least my grandfather had the decency to step in and replace your grandfather, didn't he?" Tristan countered back.

"Boys, boys!" Terry pleaded. "We haven't even ordered dinner, and you're already at each other's throats."

Tristan and I paused and grinned at each other. We had always engaged in good-natured disagreements over the years. Terry Cronklin was just not used to it.

The rain was pouring down outside the windows. It had not let up for days. Gutters were becoming rivers; puddles were becoming lakes . . . it seemed far worse than anything big brother El Niño or his little sister, La Nina, had to offer. It was more like big, bad Uncle Gordo coming down to finish the job—and finish us off!

Work had been halted on Rudolph Valentino, and there were fears that the unseasonable "cats and dogs" would wash the head away altogether! Below stood Our Father's Evangelical Church, undisturbed by the torrents of water that drenched its brick walls, pelted its stained-glass windows, and rained down upon its roof. The rising floodwaters outside reminded me, and

I pulled a folded piece of paper out of my back pocket that I had brought along. "Hey, I want to try something out on you." I began unfolding. "It's a new synopsis that I've written for my fifth-graders."

"You're doing synopses again?" asked Tristan.

"Yeah. Pastor Jeffries has no problem with them. Unlike Meece." I still said the last name only through clenched teeth, even after so many months of his absence.

"I hear you had quite a time with your previous pastor!" Terry stated expectantly.

"That's putting it mildly," I answered. "He was quite a shock after the pastorate of Milton Derringer!"

"I heard about that, too," said Terry.

"Yeah, after years of full-time ministry," I reflected, "Milton is now a full-fledged author, with his very first novel just published!"

The look on Terry's face told me he had not heard about the book, so I expounded.

"It takes place in the year 2000, and is about God suddenly sending down all of the original signers of the Declaration of Independence to Washington, DC. They get into all sorts of issues with the locals and then end up debating members of the A.C.L.U. on national T.V. I just finished a very funny part where Benjamin Franklin, all decked out in his tricorn hat and cane, comes into a local Starbucks. Looking over his bifocal glasses, he asks a guy standing in line at the counter, 'Sir, where now is your government seat?' And the guy looks at Ben like he's some Revolutionary War reject and pats his own fanny in reply! Ben looks over his bifocals at the guy and says . . ."

Two blank stares.

"Well, anyway. I'm not doing it justice. You'll just have to read it."

I felt tired. For me, the rain had sponsored a sporadic touch-and-go slumber the night before as droplets, like bombs from fighter jets, fell from high above the roofline of our home on Chestnut Street, exploding with a PLUNK! PLUNK! PLUNK! onto the top of the metal drain pipe far below at such erratic intervals that it sounded like Indian war drums beating in the distance, pounding unceasingly in my not-so-distant ears!

The supercilious, butler-like waiter came by to take our dinner orders. When he had glided away, Tristan remarked,

"I'd like to read Milton's book. What is it called?"

"Founding Fathers," I replied. After a couple of beats of silence, I interjected,

"Maybe I'll write a novel someday like Milton."

"Fat chance, Block!" Tristan pounced. "I've read some of your stuff. Even with all your big words, you are too free and easy with your abstruse creativity while using the English language." He caught himself and smiled. "We've barely sat down for dinner together, and I'm already starting to sound like you, Ian!"

Another encouraging word from Tristan Holbert, English major, against which Class Clown-Speech Communications major Ian Block was no match! Suffice it to say he could never read my journal, "Mental Ward—Prayers and Observations by Ian Block." I would never hear the end of it.

"Anyway," I looked down at my paper, anxious to change the subject. "This is from Joshua, Chapter Three." I looked up one last time to make sure I had their full attention.

"'Catch a Wave!' seemed to be a ridiculous slogan to put under the Zarethan Surfing School sign. Omar, the

owner, admitted it was wishful thinking. His surfing school could only boast taking eager students upstream on the Jordan River, drifting downstream while standing on their boards, and then paddling to the bank and carrying their heavy boards back upstream on camel back to where they had started.

"'The nearest ocean is 100 miles away!' the townspeople would say. Even in harvest season, when the Jordan swelled with flood waters, 'Catch a Wave!' was the furthest thing from the truth. One day, Omar even had to cut his lessons short as an army of 40,000 had gathered downstream on the eastern shore carrying a golden box.

"His surfing lessons the next day, however, would be historic. He and his twelve students were sitting on their boards when the river stopped flowing and started to rise rapidly. The waters were lapping right up against the Surfing School storefront and splashing through downtown Zarethan. The members of the class were all sitting on their surfboards, teetering over the edge of the mountain of water and staring down at the dry riverbed stretching out far below, when the waters suddenly gave way! Omar and his class whooped and hollered as they quickly stood up on their boards, having caught the greatest wave ever to form in the Middle East!

"Downstream, the army of 40,000, now mysteriously on the west side of the river, waved to them as they whooshed by. 'Hang Twelve!' they yelled as the surfers sped past, riding the great wave all the way to the Salt Sea.

"Omar's sign was never ridiculed again."

"Very good," said Terry, quietly applauding.

"It's a little long, don't you think?" said Tristan, ever the critic.

"Well, I'll work on it." I said, folding the paper back into my pocket, not sure if reading my synopsis so hot-off-the-press had been such a good idea after all.

When our food arrived, we ate ravenously, engaging in as much variety of conversational subjects as our chewing and swallowing would allow. Among them was my wife.

"So, how's Maria?" asked Terry. "Tristan told me about her breast cancer."

"She's doing great, thanks," I responded. "Her tests have all come back clear so far, so we're very grateful."

"That's wonderful. So, is it safe to say she's back to normal?" he smiled.

"Well, you're never the same after an ordeal like that, but if you mean she is back to her old self again, it would be safe to say 'Yes.' As a matter of fact, she is 'chompin' at the bit' [an old Colby Block expression I learned from childhood] to re-do the girls' bedrooms. She says they've outgrown the current decor. I'm more than a little uncomfortable with this, even though I know it's time. It'll really close the chapter on their childhoods."

"Yeah, we just did the same thing last year with our son, James. It was hard to take down all of his Thomas the Train stuff. It seemed so final."

"That's exactly how I feel. Like the present is becoming the past far too quickly!"

"What is all this blathering? You two sound like weepy old, maudlin grandpas at a garage sale!" Tristan could not help but chime in. He and Tina did not have any kids, so he often found cloying the plight of sentimental fathers who watch their children morph into adults in the blink of an eye.

"How's your new pastor, uh, Jeffries, isn't it?" Terry was making the most of his time in California, wanting to be fully "caught up" before he had to catch his flight home.

"He's great!" answered Tristan. "Don't you think so, Ian?" Tristan and I had not been able to compare notes on the new Senior Pastor. We had collaborated some during the stormy season of Tony Meece (which had felt a whole lot like the weather currently pounding the streets outside the restaurant window!), but everything had so significantly calmed down after the arrival of Roland Jeffries that Tristan and I had not been compelled to schedule a time together to evaluate the new arrival. The "calm after the storm" that O.F.E. was now experiencing seemed to dissipate the need for any desperately scheduled conversations that had been so rampant during the previous season of "No peace with Meece."

"Yes. Although we met Pastor Jeffries under some rather interesting circumstances," I replied.

"Oh?" said Terry.

"Yeah, we decided to take a family vacation the summer after Meece was called away. By majority vote, we selected Maui as our destination (something I had dreamed of doing since the days right after Senior Pastor Sheldon Abbott's affair with Tatiana Kincaid). We had a beautiful room at a hotel on Napili Bay. We swam, and read, and ate, and read, and whale watched, and . . . read."

Terry started to laugh. "You never change, do you, Ian?"

I smiled. "On the last night, Sharayah, who was still in the process of gaining her independence and trying to break away from mom and dad as much as possible, wanted to go sit out on the beach for a while. Maria and I could think of nothing wrong with this; the beach seemed perfectly safe—it was right in front of our hotel, and it was a beautiful night. But after an hour or so had passed, Maria decided she should check on her. She had not forgotten all we'd been through with her a while back."

Terry gave me a perplexed look.

"Some other time, Terry—that is a very long story!" To which Tristan heartily agreed.

"Anyway, after some searching up and down the beach, Maria found Sharayah, with a boy! She was more than willing to introduce him to Maria; his name was Steven. Maria said he was polite enough, but she still eyed the two of them suspiciously. Against all Sharayah's pleas for another half-hour with . . . Steven . . . Maria pulled out the 'curfew' card."

Tristan and Terry smiled broadly at this; they were both enjoying this juicy story as much as their steaks.

"On our flight home, in bits and pieces, Sharayah did confess that one thing had led to another and that she and Steven had kissed—'made out' is how she described it. We chalked it up to the tropical heat of the moment, glad that the male partner in her one-night stand was long gone!"

"What does this have to do with Pastor Jeffries?" asked Tristan, who had apparently never heard this story before.

"I'm getting to that. On his first Sunday at O.F.E., Pastor Jeffries introduced his entire family—had them all stand up in the morning service. Well, sitting right next to his wife is this boy, Steven. His name was Steven *Jeffries!*"

"Didn't your daughter find this out on the beach in Maui?" asked Terry.

"She's a teenager! She talked a little about music, he talked a little about sports, and then their lips introduced themselves! The Jeffries family was staying at the same hotel as we were. We left the next day, so we had no idea about Steven's family. Who was to know his father would be our next Senior Pastor!"

"What a small world!" said Tristan.

"Not nearly as small as Sharayah and Steven felt when both families put their facts together!"

"What a great story!" concluded Terry. There was a moment of silence, while we three continued eating, glancing around our booth, looking for more movie stars.

"Forrest Ripley is at it again," I remarked, changing the subject.

"What now?" asked Tristan.

"We came home last night to a stuffed deer head on our front lawn!" It had been a few years since any shenanigans had been perpetrated against my award-winning outdoor Christmas decorations, in particular, our plastic Santa Claus that seemed to be a vandal magnet. In an effort to dissuade additional abductions, I had grown accustomed to anchoring Santa quite securely deep into our lawn by stakes and ties so that his hatches were battened down against any yuletide agitators.

"How do you know it was Pastor Ripley?" inquired Tristan.

"Oh, it's the work of Forrest Ripley all right! I just know it. He hasn't confessed to it. I am still getting his Christian poker face when I accuse him of it at church. But I'm sure he's up to his old tricks! The whole job smells like something he would have concocted."

"How so?" Terry chimed in, also wanting to get involved in this most unique case of Christian scandal, which now included adult Bambi's stuffed head purloined from some taxidermist eager to get in on the perennial joke!

"Well, the deer head was staked into the lawn right in front of our plastic Santa Claus, and the prankster had attached reins to him, which extended to the deer. The deer also had a plastic red nose pushed down over the real black one." I stopped to chew.

"Well, go on!" said both of my anxious male inquisitors facing me.

"There were Christmas lights strung from the antlers!" I continued. The two male inquisitors broke out in uproarious laughter, much too loud for the pretentious restaurant in which we were seated, almost losing their mouthfuls of food.

"There was a sign strung around the neck of the deer."

"What did it say?" asked Tristan and Terry, now sitting on the edge of the opposite booth. I had read the sign so frequently that it had been easy to commit to memory,

"Santa, Baby! It's Christmas Eve and here you are, tied up!
When are these nasty people going to untie you so I can
once again guide your sleigh?
Children all over the world are crying because you are tied here
And they have no toys.
—Rudolph"

When I had finished, Tristan thought for a minute and then nodded at Terry. They both confidently answered back to me in unison,

"Forrest Ripley!"

"I remember a great practical joke a bunch of us played on a friend of mine back in North Carolina," said Terry, wanting to contribute in any way he could to the playful antics he so missed that were still going on with gusto in and around O.F.E.

"We got the keys to his apartment while he was at work one night. We went in with 5,000 Dixie cups and a whole bunch of staplers."

"Oh?" Tristan and I grew curious.

"We took four Dixie cups, stapled them together and placed them on the farthest corner of his bathroom. We then filled each of them to the brim with water. We took four more empty Dixie cups, stapled them together, and set them next to the first four. We stapled the second foursome to the first and filled the second set to the brim with water as well."

Tristan and I saw where this was going, and our smiles grew larger as Terry continued.

"We did this like an assembly line. One person positioned four Dixie cups, one person stapled, the next placed them in the row, and the last filled them with water. When we had finished the first row against the back wall of the bathroom, we started a second row in front of the first one, stapling the second row to the first row and so on."

"This must have taken a long time," was Tristan's comment.

"Yeah, but my friend was at work. He was a waiter in a local restaurant, and his shift lasted for hours. Well, we kept the assembly line going, completing row after row of Dixie cups all stapled to one another and filled to the tops with water. Slowly, we made our way out all the way to the doorway of the bathroom. When we had finished, the floor was a sheet of 5,000 Dixie cups all completely stapled to each other and filled to the top with water."

"What did your friend do when he came home from work?" I asked.

"Well, we were long gone, of course. But he told us later that he was exhausted from a very busy night at the restaurant, and all he wanted to do was take a shower and go to bed! It took him hours to carefully tear apart enough Dixie cups to make a path to the shower. He spilled water everywhere. He said it took him days to clear out all of the cups."

"Wow!" said Tristan.

"Do me a favor, Terry," I said.

"What?"

"Don't EVER tell that story to Forrest Ripley!"

When our plates were cleared, I brought the Manila envelope that had been sitting in the booth beside me up onto the table surface and opened it. It was the minutes to the May 12, 1933 Deacon meeting that I had discovered in my grandfather's journal some six years earlier. I had had the minutes laminated for their own protection. I handed the now stiff-as-a-board paper to Terry Cronklin, so that he could glance at my Exhibit A while I changed the subject for the umpteenth time. Or, maybe it was just a return to our original one.

"Anyway, about my grandfather. Terry, what do you know about him leaving the Deacon Board?"

There was a pause while Terry read over the minutes. During the silence, Tristan looked over at me, and I feared he was about to throw his two cents in when Terry broke the silence. What he said was a shock to both of us. He was so well-informed about the nexus of events of that fateful night that he ventilated the issues with surprising scholarship.

"My grandfather offered to help count the ballots with Morgan Pierce on the night of the congregational meeting that elected Pastor Zimmerman. Morgan Pierce shut the door in his face and told my grandfather he was not needed, that he had everything under control. Well, as you can imagine, my grandfather was a little put out! He was furious with Pierce!"

Virgil Cronklin seemed so cranky to me already when I was a kid, I could only imagine with a shudder him actually mad at someone.

"What happened?" asked Tristan.

"My grandfather followed Morgan Pierce out to his car after the meeting to have it out with him. You know, let him know how rude he'd been and all. Well, he saw Pierce put a shoe box into the trunk of his car. He decided that, instead of confronting him, he would call his friend Roy Mueller from the Deacon Board to check things out. It was a while before Mueller could get a confession out of Pierce that the box was full of 'No' ballots he had not counted and meant to destroy. My grandfather felt vindicated by Pierce's perfidy, although he did envy Farley Dobbs, the Treasurer at the time, who got in a couple of punches to Pierce's face before Ian's grandfather broke up the fight."

"So, the election was really rigged, Terry?"

"It would seem so, according to my grandfather, and we had quite a few conversations about it before he died. He was very forthcoming about the details as he remembered them. It seems he never stopped harboring his grudge against Morgan Pierce and felt any information he could leak out would continue to cast a shadow on that family."

"Not very Christian-like," I responded, hoping Terry held the same view.

"No, not at all. My grandfather liked who he liked and hated who he hated. That was true for so many men back then. Once they cast an opinion about you, it would stick, for life! And they had no problem going to church week after week with their life-long friends and arch enemies all sitting under the same roof."

"All because he got a door slammed in his face?" asked Tristan, a little miffed by the triviality of the supposed offense.

"Oh, no, Tristan, my grandfather and Morgan Pierce had been sparring for years; the door incident was just the last straw, I guess. Pierce had beat out my grandfather for a Deacon Board appointment the year before. How you do that I do not know, but he told me as much. So there was a feud going on already between them. Morgan Pierce was what my grandfather used to call a 'rapscallion.'" It was here that Terry Cronklin digressed. "You know that Morgan Pierce did not die of natural causes. I looked up the Police Record in Sioux City, where he died. He was hit from behind with some very hard object." He shook his head sympathetically. "Too old to defend himself."

"You're not implying that someone from the church—" interjected Tristan.

"Oh, no. Not really. Morgan Pierce had made quite a few lifelong enemies along the way. But I'm just saying that, back

---

then, these people did not easily forget their grievances, so anything was possible."

"You mean, some offended somebody, uh, a church member perhaps, tracked him all the way to Iowa with a baseball bat or some such cudgel to bludgeon him over the head?" Tristan reviewed the grisly details with what seemed to me a rather morbid fascination.

"I can only tell you that the Police Report was inconclusive on the cause of death. That's all. 'The Devil's in the details' and all that sort of thing." No one could argue that Terry had not done his due diligence in the case, but before the conversation turned any more like Agatha Christie, I pointed at the laminated page in Terry's hand to the last legible line before the paper had been ripped from its notebook,

"But, according to the minutes there, the Board all stood behind the vote-tampering, keeping it a secret."

"That was the pact between the Deacon Board and your grandfather, Ian. My grandfather was under no obligation to keep his mouth shut about what he knew until he made a pact with Colby Block himself."

"What?" Tristan and I said simultaneously. This was getting *very* interesting.

"I will admit my grandfather had been a bit of a conniver all his life, but he had his price. Your grandfather, Ian, struck a deal with my grandfather for his silence. Your grandfather was very concerned about his reputation around town, more than my grandfather, so he did not want any scandal attached to him. If word got out that he was on the Deacon Board at the time, there would be enough complicity to tarnish your grandfather's reputation, or so he thought."

"What was the deal?" I said, anxiously, as I waved off our butler-waiter and his dessert tray for a third time.

"Well, according to my grandfather, it wasn't a deal, exactly. It was more of a reminder of a past favor that would secure a present one."

"What kind of favor?" I persisted.

"A girl."

"What?" said Tristan and I in unison for a second time.

"All I know is that Colby Block had given up a girl for my grandfather. They were both mad about the same high-school girl, and your grandfather apparently backed off so that my grandfather could move in."

"You've got to be kidding!" Tristan responded a little sarcastically, his sardonic tone the result of the archival soap-opera now unfolding.

"She was on the rebound from *your* grandfather, Tristan!" retorted Terry. Now Tristan Holbert grew wide-eyed as the conversational situation grew more systemic.

"Who was this girl?" he said with a dry mouth.

"Her name was Wallace at the time."

At the time? There was a distant pin-prick in my memory, like this conversation was now hovering over ground already covered. I was foraging for anything familiar in my mind when Tristan quipped, "Ha! A triangle of old codgers all ogling over the same woman!"

"They weren't so old back then."

"So, did your grandfather win over the fair maiden, Terry?" Tristan asked tongue-in-cheek.

Found it! "Mental Blocks—Prayers and Observations by Colby Block, October 10, 1912."

"No." I answered for Terry.

"What?" Now Terry and Tristan spoke in unison.

"She fell for another, and married him," I said. *Wow! This just keeps getting more and more complicated*, I was thinking. Civic nepotism. Now we have another group of "Four Musketeers," this time all vying for the same Queen of medieval France—or medieval Monument, I should say!

"Who'd she marry?" asked Tristan.

"Walter Mackintosh," Terry and I said, in unison again.

"Ha! She falls for the house of usher!" Tristan Holbert said before he took a drink of water, thinking this attempt at witty parody of the late, disheveled Walter Mackintosh's decades-long service at the church and the Poe novel was rather clever.

"Cute. Very cute," I said, sarcastically.

When Jeeves brought our bill, I made the grand gesture of ponying up to pay for Terry Cronklin's dinner—not only on the pretext that he was our out-of-town guest, but that he had been an unexpected wealth of information as well, filling in all sorts of missing pieces of an ongoing puzzle. When Terry thanked me and excused himself from the booth (he had to catch his flight back to North Carolina), Tristan leaned over the table to me and whispered with a wry smile,

"Sycophant!"

HOLBERT

"Are they drunk yet?" an anxious Frank Holbert said to the "lanky drummer boy," who was peeking out from underneath the curtain. They were both nervously standing in the empty baptistry of the Worship Center at Our Father's Evangelical Church. Pastor Hale had just said, "this do in remembrance of me . . ." so there had not been enough time for the congregation to lose their memories from inebriation settling in at any level. On cue, the anemic flock had lifted the little plastic shot glasses to their lips and simultaneously gulped down the symbolic blood.

"Move over and let me see!" Frank whispered and shoved Seth to one side. He, too, peeked out from behind the plastic shower curtain drawn around the rim of the tub to scan the audience, hoping to be the first one to spy the person who staggered when Pastor Hale made them stand, slurred the stanzas of the closing hymn, and finally, being slain in the "spirits," falling prostrate on the floor while gurgling out a rousing chorus of "How Dry I Am!"

The devious idea had been planted in their bored brains by the High School Youth Pastor, Fremont "Fret" James, the nickname coming from his fast-fingered talent on his Gibson guitar. His "talk" last Sunday had been about the First Century Church in the Book of Acts and the mistaken opinion often pressed upon those early Christians of their rather "charismatic" worship behavior being the expected result of downright disgusting drunkenness.

"That would never happen at our church," Seth had told Frank at "Rudes" (a conciliatory term of endearment for Rudy's

Malt Shop, whose neon "y" was constantly burned out, or at the very least flickering spasmodically, its life-light sputtering toward complete tube darkness) later in the week. "Our church is too stuffy and old-fashioned."

At this, there was an evil grin forming on the outskirts of Frank's hamburger-chewing mouth.

"What?" Seth asked him, smiling deviously as well at the knowledge that another crazy idea was hatching in the devious mind of his good buddy.

"What if we helped them a little?" Frank said through a mouthful of meat, lettuce, cheese, and tomato. Seth eyed him curiously through his black-rimmed glasses.

"You know, gave them a little kick!" The idea detonated into details.

It was then and there, at the chrome-rimmed, Formica table in the center of the corner red booth, over the toe-tapping din of Frank Sinatra singing his brassy new hit from the jukebox, that Frank Holbert and Seth Block concocted their plan to sneak into the church kitchen on the Monday before Communion Sunday and take the cases of Welch's Grape Juice out of the tomb-like, industrial refrigerators, haul them up onto the flat portion of the Worship Center roof, and let the warm California sun do its mind-altering stuff for the next six days.

It worked for grapes. Just ask Noah, stumbling tent-bound around Ararat's first farm, drunk as the two "his and her" skunks fresh off the party boat, and literally disrobing as he goes, trying to be "fruitful" and only multiplying family complications. So, why not grape juice?

After all, 50 years ago, just a stone's throw from this very property, vineyards produced some of the finest wines in the Golden State.

Then, late on the following Saturday night, armed with Deacon keys snatched from his father, "Old man Cyril," Frank and the "lanky drummer boy" would climb back up onto the Worship Center roof and haul the cases down to the kitchen, where they could re-chill unsuspiciously. This would nicely cover the crucial transfiguration that would have occurred atop the baking roof over the previous warm days—a process that had been known 30 years ago to the Prohibition Party and the Women's Christian Temperance Union as the "F" word: Fermentation.

"When the congregation takes a swig on Sunday morning, they're sure to get snockered!"

Seth did not know if a "swig" adequately described the dropper full of Welch's Grape Juice that would be squirted into the little plastic cups by the dedicated Communion Crew, but it was a delightful thought to think of dipsomaniacal members of Our Father's Evangelical Church, "on the night He was betrayed," stumbling out of the pews, singing loudly, running into one another, and talking pure nonsense.

All they had to do now was stand quietly in the baptistry and wait . . .

"There! There's one! Holy Hezekiah!" said Frank, a little too loudly under his breath at the close of the service. A lady had stumbled quite a ways down the center aisle, but it turned out to be only Winifred Goss, the church pianist, stumbling over her too-high heels. There were no other "sightings," unless you count Mrs. Burke's wide and curvaceous posterior, two large half-moons the size of asteroids, bumping into the Christian Care offering table at the back of the sanctuary, spilling the coins from the green-felt-lined wooden bowls onto the carpet. Then, children of all ages fell to the ground like starving street urchins, frantically gathering the coins under the watchful eyes of their parents, lest the Christian Care offering come up a few nickels short, leaving certain unfortunate people, in Jesus's economy anyway, still naked, hungry, and thirsty. Over the next few days, aspiring vintners Frank and Seth could catch only scant reports of some mild headaches and stomach disorders throughout the congregation, not necessarily attributed to the Great Communion Caper.

But that is not all they caught.

"Old man" Cyril Holbert put the pieces together. An over-zealous assistant church-kitchen helper named Beulah Argyle, a wide-bodied spinster who pined for the job of church-kitchen manager and would have taken the holy spatula right out of Frances Benjamin's cold, dead hands if she had the opportunity, was not about to be hoodwinked. She relayed her story with verve to Deacon Holbert of her suspicions of gerrymandered grape juice.

"Everything was in its place, I tell you!" she told him, a little too forcefully for her assistant position. "I know every item on every shelf of those refrigerators, and I tell you that grape juice had been moved!"

Another clue came at the next Board meeting, when the new custodian Emilio Paas reported to the Board that he thought the sanctuary had been the victim of an attempted burglary. Nothing of value had been taken to his knowledge. But he had gone up to the attic one morning and had found the trap door to the roof ajar.

The third and final clue came from Deacon Holbert's wife, after doing the laundry. She noted offhandedly at dinner one night that some of Franklin's clothing was stained purple and that no amount of Tide detergent or Clorox bleach could get out the spots.

Skipping dessert, Cyril marched his boy right into his study and grilled him into a confession. After a few snippets of disciplinary conversation (like their father's favorite, "Don't you look at me with that tone of voice!") and a foreboding span of silence, there was a THWACK! THWACK! THWACK! coming from behind the closed door. Frank's two older sisters started and put their hands up to their smiling mouths and gasped at each sound. They were sure their father had unleashed his belt from his pants and was giving their little brother's behind a well-deserved beating. After all, they had endured so many fatuous and cruel jokes over the years living with such a little devil: all sorts of crawling creatures, plastic and real, in their beds, canned dog food stuffed into the toes of their tennis shoes, bedroom doorknobs slathered in honey, completely frozen bras and panties. He had had it comin'!

He was also not seen by Seth for some days, as Frank was severely "grounded," like an airplane with severe mechanical difficulty. No matter. One phone call to ex-Deacon Block from his replacement Deacon Holbert put the "lanky drummer boy" off the streets for quite a few days as well (after his own fatherly favorite, "If I ever catch you pulling a stunt like that again, heads are gonna roll!"). When Frank's term of house arrest was completed, he was right back at it again. But this time he had a target: Beulah Argyle. He was determined to get back at the portly blabbermouth for the solitary confinement in his bedroom and the swaths of red marks across his bare bottom.

"That snitch!" he had growled, glaring up at the ceiling from his coffin position on the hardwood floor. "She's no better than that Edomite tattler who ratted out King David. What was his name?" He thought through his disheveled mental files from Sunday school. "Oh yeah, Doeg! More like dog! Dirty dog!"

Beulah, on the other hand, had felt quite cleansed by the whole affair. After all, she was only doing her godly duty. It was clearly the result of her growing convictions during Preston Hale's penetrating sermons, convictions that festered into a call of obedience to finally be baptized. By wicked coincidence, an idea had already germinated in the degenerate mind of Frank Holbert on that fateful morning when he was standing with Seth Block behind the plastic curtain in the empty baptismal tub. The announcement in the church bulletin the next week that, among others, Beulah Argyle would be baptized first (disciple-dunking was always done alphabetically by last name, so Argyle headed the prospective roster), in a special Baptismal Sunday morning service the following Lord's Day, was a clear sign from heaven or the other direction that Frank's newest little scheme was meant to be.

He laid out his conspiratorial plans to Seth Block at Rudy's Malt Shop over the loud piano licks of Freddy Martin's "Bumble Boogie." Very little of what Frank Holbert devised shocked the "lanky drummer boy" anymore. After all, the tousle-haired blond boy sitting across the Formica table from him, happily munching on onion rings and sipping his cherry coke from a barbershop pole-like straw, just last year had dared to borrow a souped-up motorcycle from the boorish town thug, Travis Yoder, who had begrudgingly agreed. He threatened that if Frank even so much as put a scratch on his precious scream-ing machine, "Flash," he would beat the living you-know-what out of him! Everyone who heard this *mano a mano* talk outside Rudy's Malt Shop that night had laughed and said to one another that Travis Yoder's threat would take quite some time to carry out, as there was plenty of you-know-what inside Frank Holbert!

After years of depreciating use and noticeable disrepair, "The Funicular" cable-car system (that crawled like a red snail up and down Valentino Avenue compared to the hot-rods these days that cruised by day and raced by night up and down the boulevard), after so many decades of faithful service, was finally being put out of its misery. Once the cars had been crane-lifted and the tracks pulled out, this left an enticing wide strip of dirt that patiently awaited the renovation decision by the City Council. They debated for many long months hence on whether to put in a tree-lined parkway, terraced flower beds to coincide with the floral baskets hanging from either side of the streetlights on Valentino Avenue, or a near-vertical bicycle path with an uphill climb not for the pedaling faint of heart. The dirt—"Funicular Fang," as it was called—stretched all the way down the mountain to the bottom of the hill, where a large mound had been piled up, serving as a berm between the businesses on both sides of the street and the construction noise from a new "super highway" going in a few hundred feet beyond. The dirt trail then made a generous turn, narrowing as it curved to the right and tapering into a point, which gave the soiled stripe its wicked name, and, finally, ending at a barricade of graffiti-smattered, corrugated metal.

Around one o'clock in the morning, everyone from the ages of fourteen to twenty-one seemed to have successfully snuck out of their respective homes that night to gather at the top of Valentino Avenue, right in front of a dark-but-watchful Our Father's Evangelical Church. They would see with their own eyes daredevil Frank Holbert take Travis Yoder's "Flash" on a death-defying, careening ride down the dusty drag strip and jump the bike as high as he could over the mound at the bottom of the hill.

Not only is he going to get beat up by the fall, but that moun-tain man Travis Yoder will pulverize him for every scratch put on his two-wheeled pride and joy. Frank's deacon father will take the belt to whatever surfaces of his scrawny body have not already been mangled, was the thought in the minds of the uneasy but excited crowd that night.

After Frank snapped down the visor of Yoder's borrowed black helmet that was much too large for his head, and a few showy, defiant revving roars from the engine, the rear tire began spinning madly in a stationary position just long enough for a huge wave of sand and gravel to splatter over the delighted kids behind him. The front wheel lifted into the air like Roy Rogers' horse, Trigger, and then the whole motorcycle lurched forward. Frank was leaning into the handlebars as the machine shot down the hillside like a bullet. The only thing cheering spectators at the top of the hill saw was a cloud of dust make its way down the street, like the smoke of a lit fuse, until the bike was lifted high above the cloud into the clear night air at the bottom of the hill in the distance. Frank had hit the mound, and he and "Flash" had catapulted skyward. After a high arc with his feet off the pedals, legs spread out horizontally in the air, like a dancer doing the splits, he was lost again in the cloud of dust as the bike took a nosedive downward.

There were shrieks and groans from the top of the hill as everyone stood, riveted to their respective spots, straining their eyes, waiting anxiously for the cloud of dust to dissipate below. "Was he dead?" everyone was asking themselves privately, with bated breath, though no one had the courage to actually voice it higher than a whisper. After what seemed like an eternity, a roar of an engine was heard at the bottom of the hill, and Frank Holbert came bounding out of the dissolving dust devil, once again flying the motorcycle back up the hill and skidding to a halt right in front of Travis Yoder. Frank Holbert, caked in dirt, beamed with a sense of accomplishment when he took off the helmet.

"Where did you learn to ride like that?" an astonished Yoder asked him. His husky voice still had a tinge of bodily harm threat as he looked over "Flash," which had not a scratch!

"Wouldn't you like to know!" said Frank haughtily as the crowd burst into laughter, cheers, and applause. It was the sweetest sound Frank had ever heard in his life, but it was interrupted all too soon by the wailing, modulating howl of a police siren.

Frank was not seen in or around Monument for weeks.

"Did he beat you bad?" asked Seth Block at Rudy's Malt Shop on the first afternoon that Frank had reappeared in civilization, Lena Horne's sultry "Stormy Weather" filling the busy eatery.

"Yeah, pretty much. But I know my old man loves me," Frank said with a satisfied sigh. His miraculous feat far outshone his raw buttocks, still healing in the red trough of the booth underneath him.

"Does he tell you?" asked Seth.

Frank looked at him oddly, testing his sincerity.

"Oh, sure, all the time," he said, slightly uncomfortable at the serious turn the conversation was taking, wanting desperately to get back to his famous taming of the Funicular Fang, or whatever *other* new foibles he had hatched during his delinquency detention.

"My father has never told me he loves me," Seth responded. "I guess he just assumes that's understood by his behavior."

With the silence between them growing louder than the maddening "pitterin', patterin', beatin', and spatterin'" of Lena Horne's melodious weather report, Frank broke the barrier with an analogy that was beyond him.

"You mean it's kind of like leaving the marquee blank at the old Orpheus theatre and having the people pay a big price for admission to go in and take their chances on the movie that's playing."

"Yeah, I guess so," answered Seth, morosely, after pondering for a moment.

"Hey, guys!" A medium-height boy with greased-back brown hair slid into the booth next to Seth. The Groucho, Harpo, Chico coterie was now complete with the arrival of fellow madcap prankster, Forrest Ripley, who was famous (infamous) in secret legend among the teenagers in Monument and the threesome in the booth for being the very first to spray-paint the nose of Rudolph Valentino red last Christmas! Slightly winded from his high-stepping, boisterous walk to Rudy's, he looked at Frank. Forrest always thought the Holbert hoodlum resembled a weasel with those beady eyes of his.

"I see you've been reinstated back into the human race! Hey, drummer boy—why so glum?" he said to Seth.

"Hey, get this," Frank intercepted Seth's grappling with demonstrative father love. "One night during my prison sentence, my father comes into my bedroom, which is rare. He tells me he does not want me pulling any more stunts. He says to me that he was a lot like me when he was my age. Yeah, right! Anyway, he says his behavior cost him a girl one summer. She told him she would not stand by and watch someone she cared so much about go and kill himself."

"Really?" said both Seth and Forrest.

"Yeah. And that's not all. It was Doris Mackintosh!"

"Jumpin' Jehoshaphat! The Sunday-school teacher?"

"Yep. It was some summer fling when she first got here, and she couldn't stand all of the stunts my old man played. She was a serious one. Still is! Anyway, my old man said he liked her a lot."

"You're kidding!"

"I swear on a stack of Good Books! No Jesus jargon! God's truth!" said Frank, which meant very little, as neither one fully trusted the weasel to have a clear grasp of the facts, even if they were directly from his deacon father. The only time Frank Holbert could be taken at his word was when he was seeking vengeance, and after Beulah Argyle flapped her gums about the Great Communion Caper, which had gotten him into another go-round with his father's leather belt, he was a force of veracity to be reckoned with.

Working backwards through the twists and turns of cross-pollinated genealogies, Frank Holbert was an indirect but proud descendant of Francis Marion, better known as the "Swamp Fox" of the Revolutionary War. He had defeated large bodies of British troops with his band of guerrillas operating in and out of uninhabitable swampy terrain in the 1780s, hence the nickname. From there the Holbert line included everything: An intrepid, cunning Indian scout who led wagon trains west on the old Lewis and Clark trail in the 1840s. A trick bareback rider in the U.S. Cavalry who was stationed at Fort Laramie in the 1850s. A professional race-car driver burning up the track in the 1920s. All the way down to the son of a County Clerk for the State of California plotting his next scheme at Rudy's Malt Shop in the late 1940s.

In the foreshadowing spirit of Eddie Haskell (from that invention of the future, television, and its "real life" domestic sitcom *Leave It to Beaver*), to suit his own purposes, Frank Holbert had the dual personalities from the New Testament down pat. Not the Jekyll-and-Hyde internal struggles of the Apostle Paul from the 7th Chapter of his book bound for the church libraries in Rome, but rather Jesus's benedictory analogy from the animal kingdom that He gave His disciples on their first solo flight. Namely, that Frank had the capacity to appear as harmless and innocent as a dove at the family dinner table—and as shrewd and cunning as a snake in the hallways of Monument High.

The craze among daring teenagers in Monument those days, if you really wanted to impress your friends, was to swallow goldfish. Surprisingly, neither Frank, Forrest, nor Seth had ever tried it. They had never gone in for such cheap, two-bit carnival-sideshow tricks. They sought attention-grabbers on a much grander scale.

The Saturday afternoon before Beulah's baptism, Frank Holbert had pooled and parleyed enough money together to purchase a dozen goldfish from the local pet store. He and Seth got into the church late Saturday night and dropped them into the filled baptistry, where the fish swam about happily in their new large pool. Frank was so bent on retaliation against Beulah Argyle that he had overlooked a couple of contingencies.

First of all, for sanitation purposes, Emilio Paas always put a pint or two of chlorine into the large tub on the night it was filled.

Secondly, early Sunday morning, for the comfort of all, Emilio turned the baptismal heater on, which would warm the waters to a delightful toe-dipping 85 degrees.

Thirdly, even hardy goldfish cannot live with either.

Frank, Seth, and Forrest were all sitting gleefully in the back row of the Worship Center on Sunday morning when the plastic curtain was drawn and Pastor Preston Hale, like John the Baptist stepping into the River Jordan kiddie pool, came down hand in hand with his first, large, obedient disciple, Beulah Argyle. Both were concentrating so intently on the vast crowds giving back fixated smiles, that "J.B." and his human submersible looked down at the waters only in quick glances in order to maintain their footing while trying to descend gracefully into the dunk tank.

Pastor Hale addressed the congregation briefly, giving a crash course on the rudiments of water baptism. Beulah nervously shared her testimony, making sure that, amidst the chronicles of her rescue from eternal damnation to eternal life by the Son of God, she snuck in her concomitant passion for church kitchens and her desire to always serve in one in particular.

It was not until she had held her nose and her head was plunged under the surface in the name of the Father, Son, and Holy Spirit, that she opened her eyes underwater in time to see a lifeless eye staring back at her—a goldfish floating upon the surface! When Pastor Hale brought her back to symbolic new life, one unlucky dead fish had been caught up in the undertow and found its way into one of the many tangles of floating tendrils that made up the oil slick of Argyle hair, sticking there when she was righted. A few others had drifted into the billowy white rental robe that she wore over her blue bathing suit, and they, too, rode the wave of her re-entry.

She was screaming hysterically and shaking like a leaf. Not a Pentecostal by trade, Pastor Hale thought her remarkable reaction less Holy Spirit and even less holy water, and more like the microphone had accidentally fallen into the baptismal and that she was being electrocuted, but he quickly realized that laws of physics would have included *him* in this kind of tragedy as well. Then he saw the dead fish falling off the robe that was clinging tightly to her dripping body. He looked down to see half a dozen others bumping up against his waist. He gave the congregation a puzzled, conflicted look of trying to maintain facial control and quell his mortification while his body was itching to panic. He quickly closed the curtain and led the simpering kitchen aide out of the waters. The church organist rescued the moment by leaping into "Shall We Gather at the River?" a question the congregation would answer in the affirmative only if there were no dearly departed aquatic stiffs lolling about their knees.

Beulah Argyle was so shaken by the ordeal that she never bothered to piece together any clues about the possible perpetrators. Years later, when her dream to become the head kitchen master was realized after the death of Frances Benjamin, there was one ultimatum in her otherwise diverse menu: she would never serve fish!

No one was kidding themselves. Suspicions ran high about the Great Baptismal Caper at Our Father's Evangelical Church, or whenever anything else went awry, that the instigators were any combination of the Holbert, Block, or Ripley boys. They were given imperious looks from many of the high-handed elderly around the church campus, who often took the parents aside and offered a strong suggestion that the boys should read their Bibles and pray more. All three sets of parents found this prospect laughable at best. The boys could barely sit through a complete Hale sermon without breaking some unspoken, established church code. Nor could they stay quiet long enough for God to get in their faces to tell them a thing or two. Hope was being held out for the Ripley kid, as his family was leaving for the mission field when Forrest graduated from High School, and maybe the jungles of Zimbabwe would straighten him out. The Block boy, on the other hand, could be excused on the basis of his once-great deacon father's refusal to be seen at the church and the obligations of any spiritual training for their only boy foisted upon the sturdy but singular shoulders of dear, dear Melba. For every reason imaginable, the Holbert boy was the most hopeless case of the bunch. All three had been "born again . . ." it was just that the new creations were spawns of some anti-establishment rebellion. Much like what the "middle Son" in the Trinity was to so many when He was here on Earth.

The three would commiserate at Rudy's whenever one or another parent established a new program for subjugating them into spiritual disciplines.

"My old man is making me read a chapter a day from Proverbs!" moaned Frank. "He hopes I'll become the 'wise son that doesn't bring shame down on the heads of his parents' while I have burning coals heaped on mine!"

"My parents are using the Bible as an instrument of torture!" said Forrest, who, although innocent this time, was suspected of being a part of the Great Baptismal Caper, because some elderly church member with cataracts the size of cumulus clouds had sworn he had seen the young Mr. Ripley sneaking out of the Monument Pet Store with plastic bags full of goldfish under his arms.

"They are making me read First Chronicles 1–9, over and over again!" Forrest continued.

"Leapin' Lamentations!" said the other two from across the red booth, spasms of shivers going up and down their spines at the idea of reading who begat whom for the rest of their natural lives.

"That'll cure insomnia!" said Seth, trying to find the positive in an otherwise dismal situation. "You should have seen the way Doris Mackintosh looked at me during the piano offertory last Sunday!"

"She gave me the same look!" said Frank. He scowled in imitation of the stern, infamous "Mackface" he had received. Then a thin trace of a smile widened as he spoke, "like *we* would be the ones to stick exploding caps on the bass hammers during old lady Winifred's 'How Great Thou Art'!"

"I hear the rolling thunder!" Frank began to sing, mockingly. "Mackintosh's probably still heartsick over what your two dads put her through years ago!" said Forrest. Both boys turned and gave each other looks as if to ratify this highly probable possibility.

"I still can't get over how she looks at me," said Frank. "She drives me almost as crazy as that big Barrington boy who is always telling those obnoxious Bible stories of his to everyone he sees!"

Monument High School was one of the triplet schools built all together in the 1930s (around the same time as Our Father's Evangelical Church). Along with Monument Junior High, and the John Adams Elementary School, they served as the bastion of education for tomorrow's leaders. That education would take on a variety of forms. For Seth Block, it was as a drummer in the marching band, his tall, gangly figure earning him the nickname of the "lanky drummer boy." He paraded about the football field in his thick, black glasses, pounding away the eight counts of "The Boogie Woogie Bugle Boy," while the entire band formed a gigantic horn on the field. His mother would cheer when their halftime show was finished. Much to his disappointment, Seth's father, Colby, rarely made it to the Friday night games to see his boy. He was "gone fishin'" most weekends with his buddy, the president of the Monument Savings and Loan.

It was during Seth Block's last semester of his senior year in high school that he noticed blond-haired Nancy Benjamin from Tampa, Florida, in the clarinet section marching a few enticing rows in front of his snare. He wasted no time in asking around about this new interstate transplant. She not only played the clarinet (an instrument she would grow to dislike, intensely) like a native of New Orleans' French Quarter, but she was also a master at the accordion, like an escapee from a polka band out of Heidelberg, Germany. It was rumored, too, that her family had a large, black baby grand piano taking up half of their living room—a grand prize that Nancy had won when she was 13 years old in the Great Lakes National Accordion Competition, held in the stately ballroom of the large cruise boat bobbing its way along the shores of Lake Superior. She played the piano like a virtuoso, her style more of the "hymny" persuasion. Seth had just enough time before he graduated to strike up a relationship with this musically talented Floridian. It was a whirlwind. After the end-of-the-year high school dances, the gusts of romance further intensified over the summer months when Seth paid Nancy's cigar-smoking older sister, Sylvia, to drive them around the streets of Monument late at night while they necked in the back seat, all the while her parents, Carl and Frances Benjamin (the latter the current Palate Pastor of the O.F.E. church kitchen), thinking they were at the Palace Theater seeing a movie.

The Benjamins attended Our Father's Evangelical Church, Sylvia, begrudgingly.

Seth did notice in their conversations about religion that Nancy had an acute fear of end times. After much questioning, Seth discovered that her present anxiety stemmed from hearing a young Billy Graham preach in 1941 at the United Gospel Tabernacle church in Wheaton, Illinois. The 23-year-old anthropology major had apparently increased the numbers responding to his closing altar call by his terrifying portrait of Europe-rampaging Adolph Hitler as being, most likely, the Antichrist. Nancy never quite got over the gifted evangelist's threat that the end was very near. Sometimes this would alter her moods at a moment's notice, at the slightest provocation. After a few of these Book of Revelation date disasters—to which Seth responded in exaggerated word pictures that only made the situation worse—he decided to play up his odds of a good time by bringing along a friend to liven things up, namely, wingman Frank Holbert. Initially, Nancy tolerated this obvious "security blanket" of Seth's. But, when they all went to the San Fernando Junior College together, Nancy began to wonder if she would ever be alone with Seth again. Her only hope was that albatross Frank would get himself kicked out of junior college, which, given his reputation, was not totally out of the question.

The final solution to this unwanted Holbert papoose was sweet-and-sour, however, as Seth and Frank decided college was not for them, and they both joined the Army. Seth thought that this move would gain him vocal approval from his father. In spite of some of his World War I experiences, Colby Block was a strong proponent of the Army for every eligible male. During World War II, in the summer of 1944 (when the future deacon chairman, Samuel Caldwell, was running up Omaha Beach in Normandy), Colby himself was too old to serve. However, still wanting to do his part to help the war effort, he and Melba worked on the Ration Board at the City Hall—that spectacular Victorian architectural darling of Vista Pacifica built in 1916.

Seth waited for the fatherly approval that never came home, while Nancy waited for her man, who did. Like father, like son, Seth was stationed at Fort Ord and separated from Frank Holbert, with whom he kept in contact by letters. Since the embers of World War II had cooled, Seth filled mostly secretarial positions, honing a skill that would be essential for working in the family insurance business for which he was destined. Although, after reading a few of Frank's letters from back East, he grew worried that Frank's antics would soon plunge them directly into World War III and dramatically change both of their military futures. But their service in the Army passed without incident— international or otherwise—and both were returned safely, and honorably, back to Monument.

Neither Frank nor Seth recognized the area around Our Father's Evangelical Church in the early 1950s, as it was now a massive construction site. Cyril Holbert informed his son that the Deacon Board had voted unanimously to finally sell off the large block of stocks posthumously donated by Alma Davenport, in order to build the gymnasium and two stories of classrooms that would be the magnificent Educational Christianity building.

Fearing sawdust on her wedding dress and stray roofing nails in the groomsman's shoes (not to mention what Seth's best man, Frank Holbert, might scheme), Nancy Benjamin decided not to be married in a hard hat at Our Father's Evangelical Church, but rather have a nice, quiet family wedding in the backyard of their home in July of 1951, where she and Seth Block were joined together as one.

No sooner had the happy couple purchased a home on Vista Street, and Seth was entrenched in his new career as an Insurance Broker with his father at the Block Insurance Agency, than Frank Holbert announced his plans to marry his beautiful girlfriend, Isabel. They were the first marriage at Our Father's Evangelical Church after the construction and the very first wedding reception to be held in the gymnasium of the Educational Christianity building.

Aside from Isabel answering the same question during the reception over and over again, "How will you ever live with him?" and assuring those concerned that there was, in fact, a very quiet, maturing side to Frank Holbert that was growing more serious and sensitive every day, she mood-managed "not a dry eye in the place" when she slow-danced with her father to Eddie Fisher's new hit "Oh, My Papa!" Rumors persisted that even Frank shed a tear during the song, Isabel's proof positive that he might really have the makings of a sensitive side.

Seth and Nancy had their first baby in 1954, Owen. He was a large, solid boy who grew more athletic and aggressive with each passing day. Job, house, wife, baby—Seth was feeling the four walls of responsibility. The carefree life of his youth was slipping away with each buzz of the alarm clock, roar of the lawn mower, scream from his wife to come kill a spider, and cry from his son to give him his bottle.

Frank, too, was facing adulthood. Only he was staring it down and moving closer only by the gentle shoves of his loving wife. They had their first son, Tristan, in 1958. Not to be out-done, Seth and Nancy had their second son, Ian, that same year.

But the most sobering sign of growing up came when Seth Block was voted onto the Deacon Board of Our Father's Evangelical Church—the first Block deacon since 1933. Now the mantle of adulthood was a spiritual one as well. Arriving back home from his very first deacon meeting, he was greeted by an anxious Nancy who looked up from balancing the check-book and asked him, "So, how was it?" Seth sighed importantly, plopped down on the couch, and responded in the best way he knew how, with what Nancy would always call his "flamboyant word pictures."

"Honey, the church can be an unbroken circle of love one day and a three-ringed circus of lunacy the next!"

Seth tried to use his new church position as a conversa-tional tool with his father. He tried to talk deacon-to-deacon with him, asking him about his years at the church and why he had left it in the hopes that, like an ornery onion, Colby's soul would shed a few layers of skin. But, alas, even the son's filling of his father's shoes in this way nearly thirty years later did not entice the elder Block to open up. When he asked his mother about this, Melba simply shook her head. He noticed also on this visit to their little tan, two-bedroom house just three blocks away from Our Father's Evangelical Church a disturbing new arrangement. His father and mother were now sleeping in separate bedrooms; his green, hers pink. This, too, was given no explanation outside of the shaking of his mother's head. Their love for each other was undeniable. But love and individual space were a package deal in his father's cost of commitment. This was even evident for Seth at the Block Insurance office, where the separate, flimsy, padded partitions (that were appalling in their lack of soundproofing capabilities) situated between his desk and his father's might as well have been the imposing Great Wall of China. Had this distance between them been consistent throughout Colby's relationships, Seth might have been able to resign himself to the notion that this was just a nearly retired "old dog" working next to him who could not be taught any "new tricks," and who just happened to be his father. However, Colby demonstrated much endearing affection toward Seth's two boys, particularly his youngest son, Ian. It was disconcerting for the second generation to watch the first generation display affection for a third generation—affection that had been held in tight reserve all these years, skipping an entire generation while it waited. This was just one of the many signs for Seth that he was growing older and that playful, irresponsible youth was a thing of the past.

Even Monument was changing. There was now a busy freeway at the bottom of the hill. A tree-lined parkway running down the middle of Valentino Avenue where "The Funicular" once crept. The old Orpheus Theater was finally put out of its misery and torn down, which made the Palace Theater—now the only theater in town (evening the score with the only church in town)—all the more congested on weekends.

But this razing was not nearly as painful as seeing Rudy's Malt Shop collapse under the deadly swipe of a wrecking ball. This was to make way for a brand-new restaurant, The Rush More Coffee house, a full-service eating establishment that boasted astonishing views of the half head of Rudolph Valentino through large plate-glass windows rising from the bank of booths situated at the back wall of the restaurant.

Even the music was changing. Two decades of tunes—from Tony Bennet to Buddy Holly, from Elvis Presley to Jerry Lee Lewis—all were being edged out by more radical music that would provide the anti-establishment soundtrack for a brand-new 1960s decade. In particular, the controversial rock 'n roll band, "Stark Naked and the Car Thieves," was giving concerned parents of Monument a run for their money and allowing record stores to make buckets of it.

But the most significant change of all occurred at the top of the hill, at the corners of Valentino and Ridgeway Avenues. In particular, a Deacon Meeting at Our Father's Evangelical Church in April, 1961. Seth came through the door of their house on Vista Street after the meeting.

"You won't believe this!" he said to Nancy as he quickly hung up his hat and coat. "We voted, and it's happened!" He walked up to her, his wide-eyed face tight with anticipation, ready to pop with spectacular news. Nancy thought he was going to launch into another one of his flamboyant word pictures. But he grabbed her by the shoulders as if to say, "Brace yourself for bigger news than the election of John F. Kennedy to the presidency." He looked straight into her eyes and pronounced the three words that answered the burning question that there really was a God who was building His church in very mysterious ways!

"*Deacon* Frank Holbert!"

INTERLUDE

Teacher Appreciation Night. O.F.E.'s annual tribute scheduled to honor those folks in the trenches of ministry who have had such a profound impact on those children who become—us.

Our gymnasium in the Educational Christianity building was packed with O.F.E. tribute-payers and tribute-receivers. The Teacher Appreciation Committee had done a superb job, once again, of whipping up not only decadent desserts (including a large, chocolate sheet cake complete with an opened Bible made from mounds of fluffy frosting with the words ". . . these were written for our instruction," on its sugary pages. A "WE APPRECIATE YOU!" was added in big, bold, blue piping underneath), but also a festive environment of streamers and balloons.

Before the official program began, the highlight of the evening was walking around the interior walls of the gymnasium, where dozens of meticulously cut-and-pasted storyboards stood on tripods. Pictorial clouds of witnesses on artists' easels. Some depicted memorable moments in the world of Sunday school (like the dripping white faces from the Fall Carnival of 1993, where you could throw a pie into the face of your favorite teacher!). Others were cluttered with Bible Character Coloring Book tear-off pages showing how well children had colored either inside or outside of the lines! This year, many of the posters were devoted to the late Doris Mackintosh, the "Special Recognition" winner tonight, who would have been 109 this year.

On a table in the corner was a flannelboard display depicting Jesus, once again, mountain-topped, teaching foothills filled with vast, bathrobed multitudes. In front was a collection of ancient audio-visual equipment, including an old 1940s film-strip projector, showing off various mission fields on an adjacent screen with every "beep!" of the turning record player—all tricks of the trade of a bygone era. While looking at the spinning LP crackling its monotonous narration, my memory was jarred to a fateful summer day in our backyard on Vista Street:

Utilizing the miracle of an outdoor plug, my own, pride-and-joy record player was loudly playing, "The Story and Songs from Walt Disney's *The Jungle Book,*" while I acted out the part of Baloo the Bear, swimming lazily in our new pool (a part I also played in the John Adams Elementary School production, only to rip my costume from stem-to-stern, an embarrassing garment-rending right down the rear-end seam during our show-stopping, "I Wanna Be Like You" musical number!).

Coming home late from school, my brother, Owen, did not appreciate the poolside blaring of "The Bare Necessities," and stormed out the back door, shoved aside the needle—making a high-fidelity scraping sound like a cat clawing a trash can lid— insensitively dislodged the LP while it was turning at 33 revolutions per minute on my turntable, and Frisbee-tossed it into the pool! It sank in seconds and I frantically dove like a Navy SEAL to the bottom to retrieve it. When I surfaced, Owen was laughing hysterically as he strutted proudly back into the house. To this day, the chattering monkeys, trumpeting elephants, and roaring tigers from the jungles of India cannot compete with the chlorinated static, skips, and pops thanks to the vinyl splash-down of my beloved, long-playing record of *The Jungle Book.*

I gravitated to one old black-and-white photo from 1965. It was of Doris (still looking like an older Ingrid Bergman) standing in front of rows of children, an aforementioned flannelboard behind her with the Apostle Peter in a precariously tipping boat, pulling a straining net full of flopping fish out of the Sea of

Galilee. I was lost in memory when Maria came up to me. "Do you remember trying to sit on the girls' side, Honey?" she asked playfully. "I wonder whatever happened to Glen Tollockson?" I smiled reminiscently as Maria patted my arm, and then I wandered away to look at the other displays and chat with other yesteryear-yearning attendees.

I thought about the nurturing influence that Doris Mackintosh had had upon my spiritual youth, and I laughed as I compared her congenial affection for me in her warm and inviting Primary Department with that of Mrs. Richards, the current Superintendent of the "Come Unto Me" Children's Program and czar of O.F.E.'s Vacation Bible School. One summer, when I was no longer cute and cuddly and dipped in a thick coating of junior-high arrogance, my mother had volunteered to count money for the Vacation Bible School (her reputation with numbers was renowned, and I could only concur, what with her check-balancing agility that I had observed at home!). When it turned out to be only hundreds of pennies dropped in colorful buckets by tithe-happy children for some distant missionary in Africa, my mother decided that this would be a great opportunity for me to: serve the Lord, get off my rear end, get away from the T.V. set, get outside and breathe some fresh air, and do something productive with my life—not necessarily in that order. So, while she took on another Vacation Bible School task assigned her by the imperial Mrs. Richards, I and Nathan Raab were assigned to count pennies every morning for five long days during the first week of June.

What was more painful, however, was that we had to sit through the opening program every morning in the main sanctuary of Our Father's Evangelical Church, as officiated by Mrs. Richards, while we waited for the pennies from heaven to drop from little children's generous fingers into the red-and-blue buckets bound for Africa, which really was our cue to take them only as far as next door to the Educational Christianity building, where we would count the monotonous mountains of copper at little tables in the Toddlers Room. The highlight of the opening program for the snotty-nosed little halflings was the two mascots for the week: two little sock puppets craftily sewed and glued by Mrs. Richards affectionately known as "Fritz 'n Fran." I don't suppose Mrs. Richards thought very long and hard on the names. She must have gone with the first age-appropriate alliteration that came into her head. The children didn't seem to care, however. They screamed in delight when "Fritz 'n Fran" arrived mysteriously from behind her back on her two hands. The three of them would then tell the entranced children a Bible story and talk about some missionary in Africa—O.F.E.'s answer to Edgar Bergen, Charlie McCarthy, and Mortimer Snerd. Nathan and I sat low in our seats in the back pew of the Worship Center, rolling our eyes and cringing at the obnoxiously high-pitched voices that Mrs. Richards had so creatively assigned to the two incessantly talking socks.

After the story and offering, "Fritz 'n Fran" were just as mysteriously retired to their little puppet playhouse, and we were finally discharged from being subjected to any further corny kiddie torment. Nathan and I would grab the buckets and sprint next door as fast as our really cool junior-high tennis shoes would carry us.

By Thursday morning, we were stir-crazy with boredom. Once again, after the Great Commission's Punch & Judy Show, we ran next door and dumped the buckets onto the little toddler table and began our incessant counting for the fourth day in a row. I finished my bucket before Nathan had finished his, and

I looked around the room for some distraction to occupy me for the last unbearable hour. In a box in a corner, I spied two puppets that were heaped upon a mound of other occupational toys for tots used on Sunday mornings. The precious little ones waited for the sermon to eventually end next door, waited for their parents to remember that they were still parents, and waited to be air-lifted, like Peter Pan, from the colorful carpet to the back seat in the family sedan somewhere out in the church parking lot.

I put one puppet on each hand. They, too, were a boy and girl, with yellow and brown yarn hair and clear-plastic black eyes with rolling pupils. Nathan was still counting when I cleared my throat and squealed in my highest-pitched falsetto voice, "Good Morning, boys and girls, this is FRITZ 'N FRAN!" Nathan looked up and nearly rolled off his little blue chair with laughter. My squeaky voice only got louder and higher as I imitated the supreme matriarch of Vacation Bible School and her two little sock friends. By now, Nathan Raab was howling.

I wished right then and there that someone would have shown me a blueprint from the 1950s of the Educational Christianity building of Our Father's Evangelical Church. Cleverly, underground intercom wires were connected to the Worship Center so that those dedicated servants working with the children would not feel left out of the mainstream but would be able to clearly hear the sermon each week as it was piped into the Toddlers Room directly from the main sanctuary, and, for emergency purposes only, vice-versa! Yes, the wires were run with such forethought as to give the well-equipped "system" the reverse capabilities of relaying an Educational Christian building "Come Unto Me" Children's program emergency message directly into the main sanctuary at a moment's notice. As I was breezing through my ear-piercing roast of Mrs. Richards and "Fritz 'n Fran" on this Thursday morning to the doubled-over delight of teary-eyed Nathan Raab, it never would have occurred to me that, on the previous Sunday morning, some knucklehead would have forgotten to turn off the intercom.

The children had been divided into two groups. Some were at craft time (an unseasonable manger made out of four slices of toast was the project for today), and others were at game time (duck, duck, goose). Mrs. Richards had called together the remaining staff for a brief update meeting . . . in the main sanctuary!

The meeting had barely begun when my shrill, womanly voice filled the Worship Center with the announcement, "This is 'FRITZ 'N FRAN'!"

Moments later, Nathan's eyes bugged out in disbelief as he looked over my shoulder to the open door of the Toddlers Room behind me. Puppets (like blood) still on my hands, I turned around to see what had so instantly changed his expression.

Mrs. Richards did not think my imitation the highest form of flattery. As a matter of fact, the audio version of my parody of her simplistic puppetry and non-existent ventriloquism was perceived as nothing short of malicious mockery.

She marched into the Toddlers Room, leading a phalanx of volunteer assistants who were also wearing the same offended and determined faces of wrath and judgment.

This was no Bema seat. There was nothing Bema about the indignant face on Mrs. Estelle Richards! Nor was there any verdict. At least not verbally. I read it in the whites of her blazing, dagger-like eyes. I took off the puppets, put them back in their bin, sat down next to Nathan, and began to count some of his pennies, "One, two, three, four, five," I did not look up for what seemed like hours, until I could feel the "presence" of supreme authority, with a huff, finally exit the room.

There was a cold sweat of recall building on my pallid forehead when Patrick Hamilton called over to me. "Hey, Ian! Come here! There's a picture of us at the park with Sid that I've never seen before!"

Before I walked toward my fellow "Four Musketeer," I happened to glance at another old photo of a young Doris Mackintosh, in a cheerleading outfit, posing in front of the Vista Pacifica High School. I smiled again. I looked around the room to see if I could find Tristan Holbert to show him the photo. "He would get a kick out of this," I said to myself. But the room was simply too crowded to flag him down.

I began walking toward Patrick. I passed several other Doris Mackintosh poster tributes (with lengthy captions and articles that were more frustrating than informative, as there was simply not enough time to read them all), as I went along. Before I reached Patrick, I spied another sepia photo of a young Doris posing primly in a nice blouse and skirt in front of the mere beginnings of Rudolph Valentino. This prompted me to wonder just how many photos and slides there were "out there" circulating among the human race of people who had posed in front of our eponymous mountainside. I felt at once puffed-up with refreshed pride at the fame of our fair city.

Patrick pointed to the photo of Sid and the Four Musketeers sitting on a park bench, "Synopsis Sid" with a Bible under his arm. He was looking quite jolly while the four of us were giving the scowls of hardened criminals behind his back.

Patrick took his best shot at an explanation, "We were trying to look cool, I guess."

"We look ridiculous!" I answered. "What were we thinking?"

"In sixth grade? We weren't!" Patrick responded with a laugh.

"LADIES AND GENTLEMEN, PLEASE TAKE YOUR SEATS."

Patrick affectionately slapped me on the back as I broke away to find my family. Once the jostling, murmurs, and scraping of chairs had subsided, Pastor Jeffries proceeded.

"Tonight we seek to honor those dedicated teachers who have served so faithfully over the years at Our Father's Evangelical Church."

Rousing applause.

"But also, on tonight's program we have a special treat as we pay tribute to one of the dear departed ladies of our congregation and her legacy. We have asked several in our flock to come up and speak, and I am sure you will be blessed by the history we have been able to piece together of our beloved sister in Christ. So, without further ado, I would like to introduce our church historian, Mr. Frank Petry."

MACKINTOSH

The locomotive of the Great Northern Railway came to a hissing halt at the little Midvale/East Glacier depot. Two ladies and their male attendant struggled with heavy luggage while endeavoring to climb down the steep steps of one of the passenger cars. Walking through the steam of the engine, they rounded the side of the depot and stopped. Dropping their luggage, they looked out at the majestic log palace now under construction before them, East Glacier Lodge. Glacier had been an official National Park for only a little more than a year, and this wilderness hotel would be one of the jewels in its crown. Their own temporary lodgings, among construction and railway workers, would be suitable for at least two of the three of them to rest up before the next leg of their long journey westward.

The following day, while her mother rested, Doris and Nazareth, both accomplished riders, mounted the two horses Nazareth had rented from the Park Saddle Horse Company, and they both rode north on a day trip up to Two Medicine Lake. It did not take long for young Doris to begin complaining slightly about the insecurities of being uprooted, the hard seat on the bouncing train trip, and, most importantly, the vast hordes of exploratory flies irritatingly buzzing under her hat in the hot May sun. All to which Nazareth turned around in his saddle and said with his infectious, beatific smile,

"Demand nothin'
Be thankful for everthin'."

That's what Nazareth always said. And he should know. There wasn't a *more* appreciative person on the face of God's green Earth than Nazareth Hope. This endearing perspective colored all of the idioms and colloquialisms he had retained from his frontier upbringing in Montana.

When her Aunt Ophelia had died, he whispered as he, with his steady hand, shut her eyes tenderly for the last time. "Now she's having grub with God." Doris, to her shame, was hoping her bellicose aunt was getting the back of God's hand instead, but Doris relayed her feelings to no one. Aunt Ophelia was nuts. Mad as a March Hare. Living up to her namesake from *Hamlet*. At least that's what little Doris thought—and said as much to her friends around Browning.

"She stays upstairs most of the time," she would complain to anyone who would listen. "You can hear her shuffling around up there. Mother brings up her meals. Sometimes I have to do it, and I don't like it one bit. Sometimes at night, I can hear Ophelia creeping down the hall, dragging her slippers. Jeepers! It's just like the lady in *Jane Eyre*, Mr. Rochester's wife, who's off her rocker. Terrifying poor Jane in the middle of the night by sneaking into her bedroom and glaring at her by candlelight with those fiery eyes, embedded in a savage face. Why couldn't I have a *normal* aunt?!"

Their two-story house just outside the little town of Browning was almost too large for the four of them. It had been the result of the prosperity of their father's sprawling cattle ranch some miles south of town. The emblematic "Big W" ranch, as it was called, with a similar insignia branding the thousands of horses and cattle the ranch encompassed, was one of the largest of its kind in the early 1870s. The only problem with the spread was just that. Over the years of expanding land acquisitions, a portion of the property had swelled into what the Blackfeet Indians would forever dispute as being their rightful land. Cal Wallace would not make peace with the Indians by giving up any of the land in question that he claimed was legitimately "bought 'n paid fer." Three or four years into this increasingly vicious territorial dispute, a band of Blackfeet Indians raided the ranch one night, savagely torturing, scalping, and killing the foreman of the ranch and his family and, with their skilled bows and arrows, butchering several other hired hands, as well as burning various barns, paddocks, and corrals to the ground. Before defensive rifles could be fired into the whooping, galloping horde, they had stolen a good portion of the livestock and disappeared back into the hills as quickly as they had invaded, pouring into their secluded encampment, ready to participate in a frenzy of celebration dances and chants. One of the surviving ranch hands was Nazareth Hope. After the attack, "The Wallace Massacre," as Cal would describe it, in order to incite ill feelings against the Indians (who were "right below Barbarians and Scythians," he would say) among the citizenry of Browning, the faithful Nazareth was promoted to head foreman of the " Big W" ranch. There was none so positive in his attitude or devoted to his work than Nazareth Hope. He was an Algonquin himself, his ancestry part of the notorious Blackfeet tribe. He even had an Indian name, which he never let on to either his boss or fellow ranch hands. All because he had been given a new name now, one he said was the result of his being rescued from a "whole host of graven images." His miraculous conversion had taken place at the Browning Bible Church, where Pastor Rufus Mathieson laid hands on him and changed his Indian name to Nazareth Hope who, in turn, laid aside all of the magic, sun gods, and moon gods of his Blackfeet tribe in exchange for the Son of God from the tribe of Judah. Nazareth's appreciation for his eternal pantheism-monotheism turnabout was contagious. Anytime he heard anyone complaining, about anything, he would hold up a finger, scolding them with a smile of winsome congeniality, and say

"Demand nothin'
Be thankful for everthin'."

The Wallaces had three daughters: Ophelia, the oldest by ten years, Arabella next, and then Gertrude. To their parents' dismay, none seemed to be heading any time soon into marriage, natural or arranged. With running the ranch becoming increasingly harder on the aging Cal Wallace, and no male heirs or sons-in-law to take up the burden (about which he was quite open regarding his disappointment, using the word "spinster" with a bitter distaste), Cal sold the ranch for what was a fortune at the time and bought a large two-story house on ten acres outside of Browning. Ophelia had been an impressionable little girl who had borne witness to "The Wallace Massacre," seeing with her own eyes the horrible, gruesome, chilling images. The awful experience had penetrated her mind and festered substantially over the years. By the time their parents had passed away, Ophelia was living, nearly out of her mind, alone upstairs, while the other two sisters lived and maintained the house from downstairs—three sisters living in a macabre American version of an Anton Chekhov play.

The situation was softened by Nazareth Hope, who was still being retained as lead foreman of the house in Browning, the smiling caretaker of the home's physical upkeep and functionality.

It would have pleased both deceased parents to know that at least one of their three daughters experienced marriage, if for even only a brief spell. An injudicious Arabella finally married Spencer Lusk, a fur trapper from in and around Missoula county. However, the marriage was short-lived, as the transient Lusk stuck around only long enough to impregnate Arabella. Arabella didn't even have time to legally change her last name.

Then, no longer able to cope with the mysteriously roving sister upstairs, younger sister Gertrude pulled up stakes and moved to California. This left Arabella to raise her daughter Doris in the large house with a disturbed older sister, whose flurried mind caused her to become more and more abusive and belligerent in her advancing mental decline. She was even known to slap little Doris across the face without provocation.

These abuses Doris was recalling to Nazareth on the day before she and her mother would depart, as they sat in front of the mysteriously beautiful, manifold witness of Two Medicine Lake, framed as it was by staggering, volcano-like mountain peaks.

". . . Splendid and majestic is His work . . .
He has made His wonders to be remembered . . ."

Nazareth smiled at Doris as she spoke and began wagging his finger. She interrupted him before he could speak, "I know, I know, 'Demand nothin', Be thankful for everthin'." They both laughed, sitting there by the lakeside. Doris was really going to miss this beautiful park that she had visited so many times over so many years, with its miles of trails and eye-popping mountain vistas painted with white splashes of massive glaciers all under an enormous canvas of big Montana sky. She was also going to miss her beloved, avuncular companion and surrogate father,

Nazareth and his hope. He was going to stick around Browning just long enough for the house to be sold and for him to wire the monies to the ladies in California.

This was truly the end of their life in Montana—the last of the Wallaces and the famous "Big W" ranch of yesteryear.

The next day, Doris and her mother said a fond, tearful goodbye to Nazareth Hope, and boarded the train. He returned their waves coming from out of the passenger-car windows until the train was lost from view around the mountains, heading west to Whitefish and Kalispell. From there, their long journey would turn south along the west side of Flathead Lake, with the majestic Mission Range providing the breathtaking, mountainous backdrop to their left, and continue in such a direction for more than a thousand miles until they were safely in the welcoming arms of Aunt Gertrude at her home in Vista Pacifica.

Living with Aunt Gertrude was a complete change for the better from living with Aunt Ophelia. Aunt Gertrude was warm and very pleasant, and genuinely welcomed their company. Doris grew more enthusiastic each day about their new life in California, even with the often-traumatic adjustments at her age of making new friends and enrolling in a new high school. The present summer vacation offered a welcomed cushion in-between, to get her bearings before the school bell rang in mid-September.

"Who is that?" Doris asked of her new friend Betty as she pointed to the boy who was standing up, straddling two horses that were hitched to a buggy in front of the livery stable.

"Oh, that's Cyril," Betty said with a disapproving air. "He's a show-off!" she sneered. The other boys were coaxing the horses to walk, while Cyril balanced himself between them. They almost had the horses trotting off when the owner of the livery stable came out yelling, abruptly canceling the little circus performance.

Even at seventeen, Doris was determined not to share the fate of her mother or her aunts and would surround herself with potential husbands, however unlikely the prospects.

"He's kind of cute," she responded, much to Betty's horror. Her horror was compounded when she found out that Cyril thought the same of Doris! Thus began the most unlikely of summer romances. Doris's first impressions of the recklessly acrobatic Cyril Holbert were true enough. He was the undisputed town daredevil—equal parts of both. The three months before beginning her junior year at the Vista Pacifica High School included the awkward, clammy hand-holding in the park, that first quick peck on the cheek on her aunt's front porch, and long entries into her private diary about this dashing, rakish young man, her first real boyfriend. One day, she was the only one in the crowd who was yelling at Cyril from below to come down from a tall elm tree, where he had rigged a makeshift trapeze between it and another tree and was preparing to leap from one to another, with only a rope tied around his waist. He had both his arms pointed toward the sky, and was just about to take flight (or plummet to the earth), when "Wet Blanket Wallace" came along and spoiled the fun.

"I just want to keep you around for a while, Cyril!" she said to his deflated ego later that night while they were sitting on the red chrome stools at the corner drugstore soda-fountain counter. When his face looked as if she had just ripped out his heart, Doris tried a more godly appeal, groomed from childhood by Pastor Rufus Mathieson and the Browning Bible Church.

"You are fearfully and wonderfully made, Cyril. I just don't want you to be careless and do any harm to what God has created." Speaking of creation, she might as well have been trying to erase spots off a leopard. Cyril Holbert came right back at her with a defense of his ingenuity and temerity as groomed by Phineous Cannon from the First Christian Church.

"I am like one of those four guys in Capernaum. You know, the ones that lowered down that friend of theirs through the roof 'cause he couldn't walk, and the room was too crowded, just so he could get healed by Jesus." With this, Cyril gave Doris a satisfied air, like he had sufficiently validated and aligned his behavior with the Good Book.

"If that had been you on the roof, Cyril, the guy would have been swinging around the room in circles, like on a magic carpet, scaring everyone to death! Jesus would have had a whole lot more to heal by the time all five of you crashed to the floor! You know, one of the Devil's temptations to Jesus in the wilderness was to jump off a temple roof. And He didn't do it!"

"Yeah, but He sure had a ball walkin' on water!"

To which Doris sighed helplessly.

The battle was ongoing. In between "dates" that were becoming more and more sedate, Cyril could be seen standing on his head on a bicycle as it flew down the avenue or lying on "The Funicular" tracks and rolling off just before the bell-clanging cable car came bumping down the hillside. It was her friend Betty who told her about his death-defying back flips into nearby Brown Lake from a height she could only describe breathlessly, where he would then spiral like a corkscrew into the natural spring waters. Doris had had enough. She could no longer withstand her nightly worries whenever Cyril Holbert was out of her sight. He was sure to mature and calm down, someday, or so she thought, putting away childish things like all good ladies and gentlemen should, imagining them spiritually spayed and neutered in order to lead productive, God-fearing lives as mild-mannered adults. But woe to the girl who had to wade through those pre-nuptial years with Cyril Holbert, trembling with her feet on the ground while her boyfriend performed feats in the air.

By the Fall of 1912, Doris was single again. But her boy-less existence was brief. A friend of Cyril's, with whom was none of the life-and-limb-risking, risked extreme discomfort and self-consciousness by inviting her to a Vista Pacifica High School dance in October (after stammering some gibberish about her last name and his father's horse). Over the previous weeks, in their mutual history class, she had noticed him with an attracted eye, and so had assented. Colby Block was a quiet one, he, but she found him charming in his own farmboy sort of way. His good looks thrown in were also an attractive part of the bargain.

The gymnasium that October evening was decorated with pumpkins, scarecrows, and pyramids of haystacks, all easily attainable from the adjacent farms around town. Doris noticed that Colby eyed these seasonal trappings with a curious, admiring eye. They fascinated him. The dance's surroundings left no doubt whatsoever that harvest season was upon them all. Their admiration was interrupted by Betty, who came up for the sole purpose, Doris was certain, of a formal introduction to Colby Block, whom she had only seen, and admired, from a distance. Soon the new couple were surrounded by friends from both sides, and it was difficult to even make it to the dance floor. Doris was somewhat relieved to notice that Cyril Holbert was not in attendance. When she commented on his absence to Colby, she was informed that he was unable to attend because of a certain greasing of the high school doorknobs that left many hands pitch black, literally, all of which pointed to young, and guilty as charged, Cyril Holbert.

Colby and Doris were at the refreshment stand when a boy with a large, shriveled face like a prune came up to say "Hello."

A boy next to Colby yelled, "Hey, Pumpkin Head, you sure came to the right place!" aping the boy's looks by scrunching his face together as he spoke.

Ignoring him, Colby said, "Hello, Virgil."

"Hello, Colby." Virgil's date was nowhere to be seen, if there was one. He had apparently come up to the table for only one glass of apple cider. Colby introduced Doris to Virgil Cronklin and stood there quietly, and rather awkwardly, while the two of them engaged in a rather energetic conversation that covered a multitude of subjects, about which both were very knowledgeable. Colby looked around the gymnasium, his eyes desperate for something to do, all the while wishing he could be so engaging. Attention was drawn to him again only when he accidentally spilled his cider glass.

But that evening, when her supple lips touched his on the front porch of the Wallace home, he got the distinct feeling that he had somehow captured the heart of this gorgeous, flaxen-haired cheerleader from Montana.

During the busy harvest season, in tandem with an equally busy school year, they saw each other as much as possible. Doris was falling for him, hard. As much as she could tell, it seemed that Colby Block was falling for her, too.

They were the talk of the town. They were inseparable.

They were, in love?

Doris Wallace was just allowing this thought to enter her mind, when something happened with Colby Block. Seemingly he was different toward her—or indifferent. Her intuition told her it was not for the better. He was backing off.

He was retreating.

On the night when she felt him pulling away—and the stability of a long-term relationship drifting off into the distance—she was crestfallen and cried the deep tears of anguish and confusion. Not so much for what was telling in the relationship, but for what was not being told her. This was significantly more painful, a cup she desperately wanted to have pass from her. Even Colby's clumsy attempt to absolve her from all responsibility in the collapse of their relationship was a bitter pill to swallow. It stayed lodged in her throat for the first half of her junior year. She walked about in a state of numbness, without any logic to thaw it. The only genuine male consolation came from the unlikely source of the Pumpkin Head from that first date, Virgil Cronklin. Starting at first as the compassionate shoulder that the beautiful Doris Wallace could cry upon, she shedding Colby Block tears while Virgil patted her gently, he would then express well-placed encouragement from his wrinkled face. It was not long before they were seen together frequently around town on "dates." Doris looked tolerant, and the Pumpkin Head looked euphoric. Her toleration and his euphoria lasted nearly to the summer of 1913.

It was her friend Betty who took Doris aside the moment she first discovered the truth to inform her, rapidly gushing out what she thought was the most amazing piece of juicy gossip to find its way through their clever system of note-passing in the classrooms in a very long time.

"DorisyouwillneverbelievewhatIjustheardfromStellaabout ColbyBlockandVirgilCroklinStellasaidthatthey . . ."

A steady stream of girl talk that would have translated this way: Colby Block had been petrified at how serious their relationship was becoming, and his friend Virgil Cronklin had expressed a deep interest in the Wallace girl from his first meeting her in the gymnasium that previous October. Going against his deepest feelings, an abominable case of cold sweat and cold feet propelled Colby Block to step aside and open the playing field for Virgil Cronklin, laying down his love life for his friend, consequently rescuing Colby from the terrifying but necessary commitment and transparency now bearing down upon him. He also had it in the back of his mind that he would eventually be inducted into the Army and possibly be stationed overseas, broadening his excuses. But what also stayed in the back of his mind was the indelible impact of memories, the unspeakable joy, and deep regret that his relationship with Doris Wallace had introduced into his life.

Regardless, Virgil Cronklin had wasted no time in moving in.

When Betty had finished telling her well-informed story, Doris shuddered at the manipulation of it all. She broke up with Virgil that very evening, giving him the same lack of explanation that she had received from Colby Block. She would confront Colby someday. When? . . . As the years slipped by . . . *Someday*, she thought. Someday after he came back from the Army? After he was happily married to another? After he opened his own Insurance Agency business? After he became a respected deacon at the new Our Father's Evangelical Church? Or after he mysteriously left the church? Questions she would ask herself repeatedly on long walks around town, most of which ended up at the church at the top of the hill. As if she subconsciously knew her best answers lay there. Not sense, but stability.

That *someday* with Colby Block became *never*.

Meanwhile, time passed, somehow spinning a protective coating around the memories, softening the harshness, accentuating the warmth. Time in which had occurred the end of one World War, and the start of a new one, the Second World War receiving the biggest headlines she had seen in "The Daily Granite," the local Monument newspaper of which she remembers well the very first issue. It was from February 10, 1927, and the headline read:

"'MOUNTAIN MAN' MAX STELLAR DEAD AT 39."

The companion photo showed the architect in front of his famous Rudolph Valentino carving. It was strange to look at a photo of a man she had only met once, now dead from a massive heart attack.

During the final years of his term at Our Father's Evangelical Church, Pastor Wesley Zimmerman delivered a passionate sermon on the church that stirred her heart like none she had heard before. The timing was right, the calling crystal clear.

"There is no more powerful force on the face of the Earth than the church!" he had said, thundering at the pulpit. "The church is a lighthouse for the community, the nation, the world, that has effectively functioned by the blood and toil of millions from untold generations. It shines in the darkness, and the darkness can never conquer it. The lighthouse calls its people together from distant shores, its guiding light beckoning them to the harbor of the Rock, upon which they can either safely land, or carelessly crash! We are now the generation, gathered from all parts of this great country of ours, that is manning the lighthouse. We must make sure it shines brightly, for the sake of others seeking, and especially for our children!"

It was this last line that quivered up the soul of Doris Wallace, a pang of conviction coming deep from within her own childhood as an impressionable little girl.

She was so distraught that she did not even notice the smiling, disheveled usher who bade her goodbye with practiced bonhomie as she left the main sanctuary that day. By that evening, the effects of the sermon reached their conclusion: She must be used to help save the children. Her conviction was ratified by the light that flashed into her bedroom window every few seconds. The night of his Sunday sermon, Pastor Zimmerman had one of his congregants, who was a Hollywood lighting technician in "special effects," rig a searchlight onto the steeple of Our Father's Evangelical Church, that spun around like a lighthouse for a few minutes each evening, reminding those near and far of that morning's sermon, and of their purpose and destiny. Not a bushel was hid from the bright, rotating beam. However, after five days, the City of Monument made the church take the light down, as it was irritating the neighbors who were not so attracted to the light, and it was also blinding drivers going up and down Valentino Avenue. Regardless, Pastor Wesley Zimmerman went out in a blaze of glory when Pastor Preston Hale took over the pulpit at Our Father's Evangelical Church.

In spite of his inauspicious beginnings, one of Zimmerman's most lasting ministry reflections was that, under his waning pastorate, Doris Wallace had begun to work with the children at Our Father's Evangelical Church.

It also gave Doris more opportunity to notice the disheveled usher, originally from Bowling Green, Kentucky, who seemed to smile at her just a bit more than the rest of the folks he greeted on any given Sunday morning. She allowed him to join her on the long walks she continued to make around town. They were seen actually holding hands as they were walking by the construction site at the top of the Avenue, where the finishing touches were being applied to Rudy's Malt Shop (where, just a few years later, the "Son of Cyril," like a monster-movie sequel, would climb up to the roof of the diner on a dare and lay in the big plaster malt mug that towered above the center of the malt-shop roof. On his descent, however, Frank Holbert would catch his leg on the neon "y" of the Rudy's sign and short out the letter, nearly electrocuting himself in the process as he fell amidst a shower of sparks to the parking lot below).

It did not seem long between the time when Walter Mackintosh had first handed Doris Wallace a church bulletin to the time he handed her an engagement ring.

Thus began their new married life together in Monument. Walter Mackintosh, usher extraordinaire, the "face" of Our Father's Evangelical Church, and his wife, Doris (who bore an uncanny resemblance to the movie star Ingrid Bergman), now Superintendent of the Children's Department, helping to spiritually grow the children of the church along with two kids of their own.

It was a good life. Now that the War had ended, Our Father's Evangelical Church had built a brand-new Educational Christianity building, and a powerful new Senior Pastor, Angus Ritchie, was occupying the pulpit, energizing his congregation, with Deacon and Mrs. Cyril Holbert, Mr. and Mrs. Virgil Cronklin, and Mrs. Colby Block among them. Her hair turning silver, Doris aged as gracefully as her movie-star look-alike. As the decades rolled on, her work with the children at Our Father's Evangelical Church was still a perfect fit, as if she were always meant to be there.

She was still thinking, as she stood in front of the podium in the main meeting room of the 2nd, 3rd, and 4th Grade Departments in 1965, that it was a good life. True, there were always those clashes between her expectations and reality, the latter always overcoming and sometimes swamping the former. But Doris always embraced the notion that "it is what it is." She did not think this from a posture of helpless resignation, but rather from a prayerful assurance that a sovereign God was, indeed, on His throne, caring for her with infinite grace ever since she'd been a little girl in Montana . . . which brought her mind back to the children. Yes, the precious little children! And oh, how they grow up so quickly! She looked around and noticed two boys putting their heads together and giggling in the back row of the room on the girls' side. The tall, lanky boy with the cowlicks, fencing off portions of his tousled brown hair, Glen, she did not know. But the *other* boy—"Ian" was his name—was the spitting image of his grandfather, an old flame of hers that perhaps had never been completely extinguished.

> *"Demand nothin'*
> *Be thankful for everthin'."*

INTERLUDE

"Honey, I am going to the store to pick up the paint for the girls' rooms!"

"O.K."

"You should see the wallpaper and the curtains we picked out. You really should put that book down for once and go upstairs to help your daughters box their things."

"Sure."

"You don't seem very excited about this, Ian."

"Do we really have to change their rooms right this minute? They look fine to me!"

"Honey, face it—they're growing up. They're teenagers now. The 'Winnie the Pooh' wallpaper is just not cutting it anymore."

"I don't see why not!"

"You can't keep turning the hourglass over and over, Ian. It just doesn't work that way!"

Wow! Where did she come up with that one?

"Your oldest daughter is driving now!"

She had me there. The insurance agent's nightmare. His little girl now behind the wheel. Sharayah taking to the roads, from perambulator to Pontiac, all in the snap of a finger! Thankfully, her little sister Samantha was only riding horses (from perambulator to Pinto?), at least for now! Sharayah was even in the process of searching the Internet for a car of her own! She had already laid out a plan to save up enough money over the next year or two (she was a marvelous babysitter, extremely gifted in the care of pre-schoolers). I had to admit that her car-purchasing methods were far more judicious and orthodox than were her father's.

In my sixth-grade year at the John Adams Elementary School, Mattel "Hot Wheels!" were the rage among the boys. The male chatter on the playground was exclusively devoted to how much plastic orange track one had accumulated, how many loops, drops, and curves one had laid out in his bedroom, and how many of the precious metal cars one had collected, and which models. The most elusive "Hot Wheels!" prize of that year was the "Boss Hoss Silver Special," which could only be obtained by mail. It truly was not available in any of the toy stores we frequented. Order forms were flying into mail boxes from a good chunk of the sixth-grade-boy population that year. After weeks of mailman stalking, when the "Boss Hoss Silver Special" finally arrived, it rivaled the Second Coming (at the very least, it would surely be what Jesus would be driving when He came). Boys would secret their cars into their metal "Hot Wheels!" lunch boxes, and we would hold recess races, pitting them against each other (and lesser, inferior "Hot Wheels!" models if one dared to try to compete with the great silver terror of the orange track) on the lunch tables when the sauntering Yard Monitor with the wandering eyes had already made her official rounds and the coast was clear. "The Boss Hoss Silver Special" was the car of my dreams and had remained so six years later.

When it came time for me to save for a car of my own. I took down my black, wheel-shaped, "Hot Wheels!" carrying case from the closet and extracted the still-gleaming "Boss Hoss Silver Special" from its special plastic slot.

I went through brochure after brochure of cars, trying to match the picture with the silver "Hot Wheels!" in my hand. I would actually lay the car sideways against the brochure picture to see if the body shape was a perfect match.

To my eye, a silver Ford Mustang II Ghia turned out to be the closest clone to the "Boss Hoss Silver Special." Using this extraordinary method of consumer awareness and satisfaction, I set out at once to purchase the real-life facsimile of my sixth-grade hot rod. I was daydreaming of miles and miles of orange track stretching out on an endless Mattel horizon when I heard,

"Honey, you're living in the past!" Once again, she had me there.

"Well, gotta go," she said. "Bye, Wes!" Slam.

I gave the shut door my sarcastic "Very funny!" smile. "Wes," indeed! Of all the cruel digs! I may be dragging my feet a bit, but did she have to hit the so-called "man of the house" so far below the belt?

Maria had called me a mule. And a very stubborn one at that!

"Wes" had been his name. I made my first acquaintance with him a few days after I had graduated from Monument Junior High School, in 1973. It was to be the last of the many "road trips" I would take with my parents. Owen stayed home this time around. He had a busy summer of football practice and was quite frankly getting too old for the back-seat, station-wagon prison of the "family vacation." This last road trip's final destination was the newly completed Walt Disney World in Orlando, Florida. However, it was the brief side excursion in Arizona that had such a lasting impact and would give Maria a nickname for me that could stop me dead in my tracks. My parents decided to add a mule-trip down to the bottom of the Grand Canyon as an appetizer to shaking hands with Mickey Mouse. It was a twenty-four-hour grind down a series of death-defying, mule-width switchback trails to the roaring Colorado River bottom a mile below.

We reached the corral bright and early on the morning of our "ride." Since I was lucky enough to be the only teenager among our group, our lead Wrangler (I can't exactly recall his name. It was either "Tex," or "Buck," or "Hickory," or some other appellation to designate a person fit to git along with little dogies) assigned the most incorrigible mule in the pack, "Wes," to the youthful and callow me. Like my parents, the rest of our party was assigned compliant, docile mules that lumbered mindlessly as they descended from the south rim of the canyon, clopping along as if they had been up and down this trail a thousand times before. Wes, on the other hand, saw this particular ride as an apocalyptic death match between man and beast.

I mounted Wes with a skittishness that comes only from a previous "run in" with a mule. Literally. It had happened some six years before on a "family vacation" stopover in Ouray, Colorado. Our travel trailer had been conveniently parked next to a sloppy wire fence that marked the perimeter of a grassy field. In the dead center of the field was a grayish mule grazing absently. While our parents were setting up the campsite, leveling the trailer, and putting up our cabanas, Owen and I ducked under the fence and ran to say "hello" to the mule. Having received no formal education in Equitation, neither Owen nor myself had been warned that when a mule's ears were pinned back, it was tantamount to the releasing of torpedo tubes.

I was directly behind Owen, who was petting its nose when it suddenly charged. I fell straight on my back, and my head hit a rock sticking up out of the grass. I was knocked out, cold! It was only for a few brief seconds, however. When I regained consciousness, I was lying flat on my back right underneath the mule's hind legs. I was looking directly up at private parts straight out of a science fiction movie. The mule's back legs were shuffling, and I could hear Owen screaming. I quickly crawled out from underneath the privacy of his stomping hooves before he could do any damage to my own parts!

Owen had received only a few warning nips from the irritated mule, so the skin was not broken. But the half-circle indentation of red, the stamped imprint of a mule teeth tattoo sealed on his arms made him cry out in panic.

Mother and father came running, oblivious to our individual stories of donkey wailing and gnashing of teeth. They were interested only in scolding us for our complete irresponsibility in going up to a "wild" animal like that. As they dragged us back across the field to the lopsided trailer, I looked back at the mule. Its head was down, and its nose was undulating back and forth, masticating the tall grass. But I thought I could see amid all the crunching consumption, a bulbous, glassy eye stealing a knowing glance my way, with a gloating grin forming across his flabby lips as he munched.

My war with mules had begun. And Wes was about to bite off more than he could chew!

It was very early on in our descent down the Bright Angel Trail, etched into the Grand Canyon wall, when Wes decided to lay down the gauntlet and stop. Right on the spot. Dead in his tracks. This was not due to any obedient response to "nature calling" his copious bladder. On the contrary, he was responding to his limited intellect's rallying cry to mutiny against the burden currently straddling his sagging back. This was no Brighty or Francis between my legs—no sir, he was more like their evil-incarnate younger brother recently escaped from some donkey detention camp!

Like any freeway traffic jam, Wes's slamming on his brakes caused quite the backup of fellow mules and hikers on the one-lane trail way that switchbacked downward. After a series of these humiliating pit stops, my heels kicked into gear, like clapping pincers, gouging his rib cage while I yelled "gidday-up!" in several incomprehensible languages. The demeaning donkey-duel delays were beginning to irritate the wrangler, Tex-Buck-Hickory, who had a schedule to keep (while seated upon his perfectly behaved steed "Cimarron"). He pulled off a dead branch from a nearby bush, shaping it just so by breaking away unnecessary twigs and leaves. When his practiced, gloved hands were finished, he had manufactured quite the intimidating switch with which I was to whack the backside of Wes the next time he decided to dig in his hoofs against his unwanted passenger.

Wes's next protestation did not take long.

Once again, both four and two-legged traffic was backed up on the trail. I brought my switch down hard upon his rump, and the new sensation jarred him into obedience. It also temporarily stroked my own ego, as I was now the consummate cowboy, able to tame wild beasts and show them who was boss. Every time Wes dared to halt his bulky self on the trail—WHACK! Another stinging incentive from Cowboy Block! Halt. WHACK! Halt. WHACK! Halt. WHACK! We went down the canyon trail with the fits and starts of an old, backfiring jalopy. When Wes's backside was completely numb, his burro brain decided on plan B. It had *mafia gangster* written all over it. "Rub the guy out." Literally.

The gaping maw of the Grand Canyon rim, like a wide fun-nel, now narrowed into the more precipitous drops closer to the raging Colorado River. The precarious footpath presented the rider, who was blindly trusting the instincts of his stumbling transportation, with three options. One, follow the two-foot-wide rocky route as marked. Two, fall to the right to certain death 3,000 feet below. Or, three, scrape yourself raw against the craggy cliff wall to your left.

Wes chose for me option #3.

As I whacked him now with the frequency of a metronome, he slyly moved his body to the extreme left side of the trail as he made his way down. This put me in direct contact with the razor-sharp rocks and wickedly thorny mesquite bushes indigenous to any canyon wall in the Southwest. After only a few hundred feet of Wes's "leaning on me," my left pant leg was in tatters. My leg, arm, and elbow were scraped and bleeding. His mangy head was hanging down in mock subservience to the yoke of slavery, but I am sure, if I could have seen his ugly face, Wes would be cracking that gummy smile, showing off a row of yellowed, dull, flat teeth at the methodical raking of his unwanted passenger.

WHACK! WHACK! WHACK!

"Sorry, cowboy," Wes seemed to say, "I can no longer feel a thing back there!"

After seeing my shredded left side on our lunch stop halfway down the canyon, Wrangler Tex-Buck-Hickory came to my rescue once again. This time, he took out his knife, pulled up a good, stout limb of birch, and began whittling nimbly. When he had finished, he handed me a sharp, pointed wooden scalpel about five inches long.

"If Wes starts to act up again, jab this here goad into the side of his neck. That's where his nerves are. That'll git his attention."

Goad. There it was! Tex-Buck-Hickory had said the word. *Goad.* Right out of the Bible! The very means that almighty God uses to get the point across to people who are bucking the system was now cradled in my hand! I tried to smile like God would have. Benevolently. Always seeing the greater good of humankind. But my smile came out only sinister, vengeful, anxious for retribution.

At this stage of our journey, the furious Colorado River rapids were a straight drop down thousands of feet on the right side of the trail. Wes did not waste any time pinching me against the canyon wall to the left. I drove the goad home. Wes's neck muscles fluttered, and he moved immediately to the center of the narrow path. A couple of jabs to the neck, and Wes was domesticated. The wild beast was tamed by a man who walked medium height and carried a sharp, little stick. Four hours later, we crossed the footbridge over the Colorado River and headed into a cluster of cabins that were our final destination, Phantom Ranch (probably named after those dearly departed spirits who were not able to stay on their mules!). After a family-style dinner in the dining hall, my mother, father, and I went to bed, exhausted. Our sleep was sound and deep. Bow-legged, but sound and deep.

The next morning, after a hearty breakfast, I walked over to the split-rail fence that formed the corral around the mule pack. I came up to Wes, who was eyeing me. Like the Grim Reaper's sickle, I pulled the goad out of my pocket and showed it to him, brandishing it with ghoulish delight. His neck was still red from the day before, which kept his memory intact. While shaking the stick in his face, I moved my mouth to his pinned-back ears and said, "Make one bad move, pal, and, so help me, I'll stick you to kingdom come." Not much left of the Lord's Prayer, but very effective with a stubborn animal, the *ass* so common in the Bible.

For the next six hours, Wes carried me without incident back up safely to the south rim of the Grand Canyon—thanks to the pin-pointed encouragement wrought by that marvelous invention, the *goad*.

Maria had browsed the Kodacolor diary many times that served as an accompaniment to my oft-repeated but never-embellished story of my adventures with Wes. Nowadays, the name of the mule in the fading photos of the album had become Maria's recriminating reminder to me whenever I flashed her my stiff neck.

Even good ol' King Solomon, after concluding that there was nothing new under the sun, at least had to admit that his wise words were as good as *goads*. Only a man with 1,200 horses to his credit could know that, even if he had never ridden Wes.

Sigh. "Now, where was I?"

I looked down at the book in my lap. Milton Derringer's first novel was really re-charging my political batteries, energizing the Judeo-Christian soapbox upon which my feet were securely nailed. To that end, I returned to its pages once again.

"Conrad Baines opened the session by calling for order within the great, historic Senate Chamber in the Capitol of the United States of America. His voice echoed in the cavernous hall. The original colonists sat staring at him, none of whom showed even the slightest wince of intimidation, remarkable given the fact that they were surrounded by microphones on booms, hot, bright lights with reflector screens, and a dozen television cameras representing stations from all over the world, technology that would have missed them by more than 220 years. Thomas Jefferson leaned back with his arms folded, whispering to John Adams. His dress was slightly disheveled, like he had just come out of his self-imposed quarantine from the upper room in Philadelphia where he was rewriting drafts that would rewrite the ideals of human self-government, lifting it to a whole new level never before

attempted. George Washington, on the other hand, was all decked out in pressed military garb like he was ready to re-cross the frozen Delaware River. He sat properly at his desk, immovable, always looking forward to the front podium with a fixed stare. A frustrated Benjamin Franklin was the last to take his seat, his inquisitive conversation with a cameraman cut short by the shrill feedback from the lectern microphone. Of the representatives from the past, George Washington and Thomas Jefferson were elected as spokesmen for the debate against Conrad Baines and Fran Collester, the former a respected spokesperson for the American Civil Liberties Union, and the latter one of their most prized attorneys. The other Signers of the Declaration of Independence, Samuel Adams, John Hancock, Benjamin Harrison, and some 50 others were seated throughout the hall, or standing against walls, along with their 20th- and 21st-century spectator counterparts. Television-crew men had raised their hands, giving the five, four, three, two, one, countdown as red lights came to life in synchronization on the scores of cameras. This seemed to be the moment for which the medium of television had been invented 50 years earlier: To capture this exchange of ideas in a forum that would be indelibly etched in the minds of millions of viewers like no other event in modern history. Two schools of thought that had been on a collision course since their divergent inceptions, the "experiment in freedom" from the older one inadvertently spawning the younger other, were about to compare notes. No one was going to miss this for the world. In fact, it seemed to be for the sake of the world that all had tuned in.

"The event had been preceded by the expected protests and sidewalk debates, with both the Metropolitan Police

Department of the District of Columbia and the United States Capitol Police making more than a handful of arrests. Picket signs were bobbing up and down in the crowds from both sides of the fence. Even an outspoken preacher stood on a large wooden soapbox on Pennsylvania Avenue in front of the White House with an inscription from Proverbs 22:28 painted on the side of the box,

'Do not move an ancient boundary stone set up by your forefathers.'

"*During introductions, Mr. Baines addressed Washington as 'Mister President,' which surprised some by its deference and courtesy not common in any of Mr. Baines' argumentative discourses. Perhaps he was just buttering up what he would shortly turn into toast. He surely would not disappoint those who had come to admire him as the supreme liberal advocate for human rights. The podium was then given over to a sullen, impeccably dressed-in-navy-blue-business-suit-with-tightly-pulled-back-hair Ms. Collester, who read the previously agreed-upon rules of conduct and order, in particular admonishing the capacity crowd seated in the gallery above to behave themselves. Security was tight. Guards were everywhere. If anyone got out of line, extraction was assured, swift and permanent. And the debate was on.*

"*Ms. Collester wasted no time in going after the heart of the matter and dropping the 'Mr. President' title to prove it. Looking directly at the first president, she stated,*

'Let us first explore this idea of our being a 'Christian Nation' as supposedly espoused by you and your fellow 'Deist' antecedents, shall we?' (Ms. Collester's exaggerated emphasis on 'Deist' and 'Christian Nation' caused a sweep

of frowns and more folded arms from the original colonists, correctly sensing that their hearts and minds had been locked in punishing stockades, their concepts of God pigeonholed into something all too convenient and simplistic. At the very least, these A.C.L.U. folks did not know their history!) The intonations in her speaking manner, as if there were a foul taste swishing around in her mouth, clearly indicated that she and the organization she represented thought the very idea of a Christian Nation preposterous, fallacious and repugnant. 'First of all, do you consider yourself a Christian?'

"There was an audible gasp throughout the chamber at the forthrightness in tackling such an uncomfortable, personal issue, but Ms. Collester did not flinch or change her expression in any way to soften the motive behind her question. With a furrowed brow, George Washington looked down at the microphone pointed at his face on the desk, eyeing it curiously. He was a bit surprised by the amplification in his voice when he leaned forward and heard himself clear his throat.

"'Madam, I take a particular pleasure in acknowledging that the interposing Hand of Heaven has been most conspicuous and remarkable.' He smiled affably and confidently.

"'Yes, but do you consider yourself a Christian?' Fran pressed the first President, not returning the affable smile.

"George Washington took a deep breath, as if to gather enough steam to accurately ventilate his heart, 'In Jesus Christ I acknowledge and confess. Jesus Christ the Way, the Truth, and the Life. I know my sins are forgiven by His death and passion. So into Thy hands I commend myself, both soul and body.'"

172

I remembered from a recent email conversation with Milton that he was determined to have his Founding Fathers utter their exact words. So, aside from biblical references, Milton used only direct quotations from historical documents for this debate.

"There could be detected a slight smirk on the face of Fran Collester, as if she could not believe the imbecility coming from the lips of the supposed Father of Our Country. She thought smugly at how wrong we had all been in giving this man that title, not only for his unstable religious views, but also for the fact that he was proven impotent and could not physically have any children of his own!

"'Do you think, sir, that this is a proper perspective for a president to embrace? Are you really equipped to soberly lead a country with such a religious dependency?'

"'No country upon Earth ever had it more in its power to attain these blessings. Much to be regretted, indeed, would it be, were we to neglect the means and depart from the road which Providence has pointed us to, so plainly.'

"Thomas Jefferson whispered into Washington's ear, giving him a quick rundown of what he had discovered in the Capital city during the past week about the growing antipathy between religion and the nation's government, and the scorn voiced by so many of its people, to which Washington said to Jefferson, clearly, into his own microphone,

"'I cannot believe it will ever come to pass. The Great Governor of the Universe has led us too long and too far . . .'

"'Mr. Washington,' Ms. Collester resumed. But the President continued speaking,

'It is the duty of all nations to acknowledge the providence of Almighty God, to obey His will . . .'

"'Mr. Washington! If you please!' Fran's curtness did not curtail the fervor and passion of the tall man from Mount Vernon.

"'. . . to be grateful for His benefits, and humbly implore His protection and favor . . .'

"'Mr. Washington!' She was now demanding, not the slightest hint of supplication. The first president stood up from his desk against the impertinence he perceived at these interruptions. A trickle of sweat from the hot lights slid down the side of his taut face. The audience was riveted with an anxious hush both live and in living rooms. It had not taken long for tempers to flare and passions to rise between these two radically opposed institutions of Puritanism and paganism.

"'It is in an especial manner our duty as a people, with devout reverence and affectionate gratitude, to acknowledge our many and great obligations to Almighty God, and to implore Him to continue and confirm the blessings we experienced.'

"'So, do you believe in the separation of church and state?' Conrad Baines interjected, leaning into his own microphone.

"'Of all the dispositions and habits which lead to political prosperity, religion and morality are indispensable supports.'

"Affectionately calling him by his Indian name, 'Caunotaucarius,' Jefferson gently grabbed Washington by the arm in an effort to seat him once again and to take the floor himself. To that end, he, too, stood up.

"'The Christian religion, sir, is a religion of all others most friendly to liberty, science, and the freest expansion *of the human mind. Religion, morality, and knowledge being necessary to good government and the happiness of mankind, schools and the means of education shall be forever encouraged.'*

"'So you would have us believe that it is your intention that everyone in America be a Christian, like yourself?'

"There was a voice heard from the back of the room, Cameras instantly whirled around, and microphones shifted directions, locking onto the adamant words of a standing Benjamin Franklin,

"'A Bible and a newspaper in every house, a good school in every district—all studied and appreciated as they merit—are the principal support of virtue, morality, and civil liberty.'

"By their faces, the two representatives of the A.C.L.U. were taking umbrage at Mr. Franklin's jibe at part of the title of their organization, especially his connecting it to any religious document. Jefferson turned back around to face his opponents.

"'The whole American people declared that their legislature should make no law respecting an establishment of religion, or prohibiting the free exercise thereof, thus,'

"'. . .and to think we carved your heads in stone out in South Dakota!', yelled a voice friendly to the A.C.L.U. from the top row of the gallery. He was immediately apprehended by security guards and was still screaming at Washington and Jefferson while he was forcibly escorted from the Senate Chambers.

"The two Founding Fathers stared at one another quizzically at the odd reference to a stone carving. An efficient aide quietly came up behind them and placed a

color photograph on Jefferson's desk of Mount Rushmore. The two stared down at the picture of the Monument in disbelief. Then Jefferson smiled broadly, leaned over, and said to Washington in a whisper words from Jesus that were picked up only later by the Network News when the audio tape had been replayed and the sound enhanced,

"'If these should hold their peace, the stones would immediately cry out.'"

STELLAR

Maximillian loved to play with rocks. Not the usual array of tin soldiers or toy cars with which the other boys played. No. Just rocks. It had been six years since Grover Cleveland and Benjamin Harrison had duked it out for the White House. But political stages and their actors were the furthest thing from Maximillian's mind. In their rural home outside of Grand Rapids, Michigan, he felt quite secluded from the national events of 1895. His life consisted of chores, school, family, and, for recreation: Rocks.

He collected all kinds. Some were found around his home, others by the shore of Lake Michigan, and some were given to him by friends and relatives from their own discoveries and travels, as they sought to contribute to Maximillian's penchant for the Stone Age. Coming in all shapes and sizes, some were speckled, like hens, and some were striped, like raccoon tails. Still others were as black as panthers, or white as doves, some nearly as clear as liquid, some as porous as honeycomb. As Max's petrology collection grew, the wooden box underneath his bed became more and more of a chore to slide in and out, as it became heavier with each additional entry. It was even more of a feat to heave the hefty container up onto his bed to examine and re-examine his precious possessions. He could spend endless hours inspecting them, examining their intriguing patterns in the streaming light of his little bedroom window. Or he would place them in piles of like kind and quality, and have rock wars between armies. Smooth quartz against ivory agates, igneous pumice against solid granite, hardened clay against soft seashells. He would still make the boyish sounds of artillery and cannon fire, but the strange clicking sound heard beyond his closed bedroom door would not be the clash of tin bayonets or muskets of foot soldiers in hand-to-hand combat, but rather the crack and thud of pebble platoons, boulder brigades, gravel grenadiers, and marble militias being pitted against one another.

The epiphany came when Max was around eight years old. The Granite War being fought on top of his bedspread was reaching a fever pitch. The David rock from the Upper-Pillow-Side Army was in combat with the Goliath rock from the Lower-Foot-of-the-Bed Army. Kneeling in praying position, with his knees on the hard, wooden floor, Max grabbed both of his prized pieces and slammed them together in one last battle for total bed conquest. The final collision of the two warriors proved a tragedy for the Lower-Foot-of-the-Bed-Army. While the David rock remained dazed but intact, the Goliath rock had been mortally cracked, and then broke into diversified chunks and nuggets right in the palm of Maximillian's hand. When the initial surprise and disappointment that one of his most coveted collectibles had been diminished to humble fragments wore off, he looked again at the granite body parts arranged on his outstretched hand, as the sun shining outside his window tossed just enough light and shadow on the odd shapes and sizes to give them a whole new life and appeal. Maximillian stared in fascination, tilting his blue eyes and rerouting his head around his frozen palm to see all angles of his decimated Goliath rock. He did not see the Bible's many Philistine permutations from the famous giant's progeny, with their looming spears and sextets of fingers and toes. Rather, Max's imagination took flight as the new shapes became the faces of birds, animals, people. Now he could see brand-new worlds revealed in the busted fragile bits and pieces that could not be seen when it was a smooth, intimidating whole.

He ran out to show his mother, who was shucking corn with his younger sister. His father, mother, and sister had often wondered why the reclusive Maximillian exhibited none of the developmental qualities of other children in the area. When he was spotted around the neighborhood kicking the ground, looking for more additions to his collection, the other boys would taunt Maximillian, yelling that he truly had ". . . rocks in his head!" Maximillian showed no signs of caring about this form of persecution—particularly now that the smashed Goliath had been reborn into fantastical smithereens.

His next quest was for the sharpest piece of flint that he could find. His father was the one who discovered it while they were removing a tree stump from the backyard. "Look, son, it's an Indian arrowhead! Probably from the Ottawa tribe!" Max, however, would not calm his father's unease by becoming "normal" and playing cowboys and Indians with the other boys as a result of the find. On the contrary, every free moment he had, Max was using the flint as a primitive tool to chip away at whatever rocks in his collection would give way, carving rough-hewn, vague shapes whose identity was solely the mental property of Maximillian Stellar.

When he received an actual carving chisel for Christmas, Max was off and running to find more rocks in the woods for his collection. This time they would not be privates, colonels, or generals in the great war upon the bedspread, but rather conscripted raw material for experiments "under the knife," subjected to the carving and chipping that was driven by the imaginative whims of Surgeon Stellar. The igneous, sedimentary, and metamorphic were his template, all three trying to remain inconspicuously buried in the waiting room of the woods behind his house.

Soon there was a growing collection of Maximillian's ingenious creations lining the wooden shelves in his bedroom; elegant swans, playful bears, soaring birds carved with the deft precision of an artist's eye. His family began to take notice and marvel at the hidden talent deeply imbedded in this unlikely boy, a gift that had been quarried and exposed at this particular time by a Higher Power in much the same way that little Max worked his eyes, hands, and chisel into a dance whose cadence produced what his family was soon to admit were little masterpieces of sheer genius . . . raw, diamond-in-the-rough talent that had now been allowed to flow out of him and shine.

In a natural progression of budding commercialism, Max began to sell his little animals to neighbors and friends in and around the Grand Rapids area. When it was becoming quite the humming business, Max's father came into his room one night and philosophically hit Max's artistry with the sledgehammer of practicality.

"You can't make a decent living off carving cute little animals, son. You need to find a trade that will keep clothes on your back, food on the table, and a roof over your head—like I've done."

Max looked around his room and, picturing the meager living space of the surrounding house beyond, deduced even at his young age that his father had, in fact, stepped up to the plate as provider for his family, but had only bunted. His mundane job in the textile mill did not allow him to hit any home runs or even a respectable line drive. Their existence was adequate but scant by Max's standards. Over time, his criticism of their home blossomed into downright frustration. He possessed and pampered persnickety thoughts of how much better he could have done: A larger kitchen for his mother, a more direct route to the bathroom, a bigger bedroom for himself, and, yes, if she really complained loudly enough, a bigger bedroom for his sister as well. And, more distance between his, his sister's, and their parents' bedroom, so they did not have to hear mom and dad talking, laughing, arguing, or whatever else was going on in there into the deep hours of the night.

This symptomatic criticism eventually revealed its root cause to Max: creativity.

"I'm going to become an architect!" he told his family after many months of mental pondering and pounding against physical walls that should not have been there. With the propulsion that comes from the pride of parents, Max was enrolled in classes and learned the academic rudiments that would rocket him into his career of choice. His father thought that his innovation to become an architect in this vicinity would be a sure-fire success due to the high volume of furniture manufacturing that had already made their city quite famous.

Even though his father had blacklisted "sculptor" as a laugh-able means of self-sufficiency, Max still collected and carved stones every free moment he could lay his inventive hands on. He obtained books from the local library on Michelangelo, Donatello, and Bernini, and, in addition, read current events on budding sculptors like Auguste Rodin. Soon his stone menagerie was increasing in size as larger blocks were procured. Now the front and back porches and the yards resembled a frozen zoo.

But the greatest opportunity came when Percival Scott came to call on the Stellar family with a proposition for Max.

"The City has at its disposal an acquisition of funds designated for a memorial which is to be located in Jefferson Park—on the hill overlooking the duck pond, to be precise. We would like very much if one 'of our own' would do the honors of sculpting a statue for the memorial. We simply cannot pay the exorbitant commissions of the more-renowned artists. The City Council has agreed that young Mr. Stellar here would be more than adequate to the task. Members were even passing around samples of Max's highly original work that they had purchased over the years." He looked straight at Max and said, "You only need to submit your sculpting ideas to the City Council for approval, son. We will supply the materials."

Before his parents agreed, the family toured the site of the proposed memorial in Jefferson Park. They were won over by the lush serenity of the surroundings, the little knoll where an octagon of crude sawhorses was positioned to cordon off the intended area, and they were convinced that Max should take on his first official commission. This would put his architectural education on hold for the duration, but Max agreed to return to his studies with renewed fervor the minute his statue was revealed.

He hit the books immediately, looking for possible ideas for the historical memorial. After numerous submissions, the City Council voted unanimously on his idea of two figures, standing back to back. One would be Louis Campau, the French settler who founded the first trading post in 1826. He would be holding up in his hand a pelt of fur, as if in offering to an invisible customer. The other figure would be that of Isaac McCoy, the first white settler from 1825 and Baptist preacher, who would be standing behind his pulpit with his finger pointing at an imaginary congregation.

A cart drawn by four horses was soon seen creaking its way up the dirt driveway to the Stellar house, the driver halting the exhausted bays at the backyard. It took four grown men (the driver, his father, and two neighbors curious enough to follow the mysterious cart to its destination and soon finding themselves strong-armed like Babylonian war captives into slave labor!) plus Max to maneuver a large, fairly rectangular block of granite that was three times the size of Max. It was plopped onto the ground with a dull thud that forced a six-inch indentation into the tuft of grass upon which it landed. They successfully rolled it over twice so that it rested on the wooden plinth Max and his father had erected in preparation for the block's arrival.

Max set up ladders on all four sides, tented the area against inclement weather, gathered his collection of tools, and began to work on the memorial. The chinking and chipping could be heard around the clock, and no one was permitted into the backyard for six long weeks.

Finally, after weeks of neglected meals, strained muscles, and forgotten chores, Max Stellar found himself sitting in a chair on top of a red, white, and blue bunting-skirted stage in Jefferson Park among an intimidating row of City officials, dignitaries, and even the Governor of Michigan, all present for the unveiling of the memorial.

After more laudatory comments than a young mind could humbly digest, Max climbed the ceremonial ladder next to his veiled creation and announced as he pulled back the black tarp,

"I give you our Founding Fathers!"

A breeze caught the tarp as Max was lifting it, flapping back and forth to expose, in teasing intervals to the large, standing crowd, glimpses of two sets of feet, then legs, and finally trader Louis Campau offering his pelt, and minister Isaac McCoy pointing his finger for eons to come on the little knoll overlooking the duck pond.

The crowd exploded with applause of awe and approval. Max stood there on the ladder, gracefully dipping his head in a respectful bow and blushing ever so slightly.

He was on his way.

But not until Max's parents made him make good on his promise to finish his courses in architecture. Max eventually graduated with a degree in architecture and actually began his trade working as an apprentice in a firm that specialized in designing and redesigning homes for the affluent in and around Grand Rapids.

But every chance he had, he would return to the knoll overlooking the duck pond and look up into the insightful eyes of his two determined pioneers and ask them both, "Is this all there is?"

His family were staunch Catholics, at least on paper. Only dipping their toes into the fringes of their religion of tradition— preferring to treat the safer ceremonial trappings as indispensable rather than squeezing into a completely committed, penitential confession booth. Religion to them was just one piece of many in a child's puzzle, rather than the frame that holds all of the adult pieces together.

Even so, Max had inherited a concept of God. So, without the clarity of any priestly counsel, he looked into the eyes of the two graven images of his own making, seeking guidance from the faces that seemed to see with great confidence far beyond the knoll, the duck pond, to an endless horizon brimming with opportunity, a vista tapping Max on the shoulder, but staying just out of his reach. Max still kept abreast of the sculpting world and its stars—the achievements, disgraces, camaraderies, and dissensions of the likes of Rodin, Borglum, Saint-Gaudens.

Sitting on his bed one night, thumbing through the colorful sculpting journal in his lap, Max's eyes grew two times their normal size when he looked at a picture of a huge, granite dome sticking up from the woods like a prehistoric turtle laying in a bed of green undergrowth. He scanned the article, looking for the name of the petrified beast. Stone Mountain. His wide eyes moistened as if salivating over the potential canvas this monolith offered. He continued reading. One of the nation's sculpting stars had already seen what Max had seen and had been commissioned to carve a complex Civil War memorial on the side of the mountain. Included was an early artist's sketch of the completed work: Renowned Civil War generals riding on horses—a massive undertaking for even the most accomplished of artists.

"He's going to need some help," Max said flatly to himself, closing the magazine and walking obediently, as if transfixed by a higher calling, into the living room to enlighten his parents.

The request to go to Atlanta, Georgia, was firmly denounced as folly by both his mother and his father. Both wanted him to marry, settle down, and ply his architectural trade for the rest of his life. "A stable, but boring existence even on a good day!" was Max's voiced opinion.

But practicality versus potential remained at an impasse. Family dynamics became awkward at first and then grew tense as Max fell into the role of a caged animal, like so many he had carved, trying to break away from the family fetters he had now lived with for a quarter of a century—links of chain that had voices of their own as they calibrated the consequences from the safety and security of Grand Rapids, Michigan:

"Where will you live?"

"What will you do?"

"How will you eat?"

and celebrated the complacency of staying put,

"Why don't you find a nice girl here in town?"

"You have a perfectly good job with your firm."

Predictability had its own special brand of tyranny. A cocoon of what was expected wrapped around Max, the straitjacket of normalcy. The constriction grew suffocating. At times, Max felt as if he were only one stray thought away from insanity. Like a cow in a rodeo, one foot and then the other stepping into the lasso, the ropes yanked and the cow roughly flipped over on its back. Third and fourth legs lassoed, and a rope is finally thrown around its oscillating neck for what . . . strangulation? No. It is not put out of its misery. It suffers a worse fate. A hot, searing brand is symbolically burned deep into his flesh: PREDICTABLE.

Since his family had not personally introduced him to a friendly God to bounce things off, Max again turned his mind to the two granite faces in the park. While he appreciated the wide assortment of sainted statuary of Catholicism, they seemed to hear only what was memorized (liturgy) and only at a time (mass) and place (cathedral) of their own choosing.

Standing on the knoll in Jefferson park and looking up at his creation, was it more than coincidence that the two back-to-back men had their heads turned, both facing southeast? He stared longingly at the two faces he had engraved, hoping he had chiseled answers for himself in their expressions. Just then the words of Michelangelo came to mind, as if, together, Mr. Campau and Mr. McCoy were whispering in his ear,

"I saw the angel in the marble and carved until I set him free."

Over the ensuing weeks and months, Max survived by advancing all of the news to his family that was swirling around the great mountain in Georgia. The chain links of opposition began to show signs of rust, weakness, and decay. Neighbors and friends corroborated with overwhelming unanimity that Max Stellar should go and "lend a hand, uh . . . chisel!" to that flat side of Stone Mountain.

The Stellar family chain eventually broke apart, individual links clinking reluctantly to the floor. Out of the dismal pile of practical dreams for their son emerged a lopsided Maximillian, two suitcases in his hands, one full of essential clothing and sundries, the other much heavier, with even more essential samples of his stone carvings over the years—rock resumes.

He bade his family a fond and grateful farewell, and dragged his two suitcases by riverboat, steam train, and hitchhiked wagon to the steaming humidity, Spanish moss, and the giant, petrified tortoise shell in central Georgia. On July 20, 1916, 27-year-old Max Stellar first laid his eyes upon Stone Mountain. It had been a full two months since the commissioning ceremony for the Confederate National Memorial, and already there were workers, like so many ants, erecting stairways and platforms in preparation for actual carving.

With only a pittance left of his savings, Max quickly made his way to a feeble shed that looked to be an office at the base of the mountain, to inquire about a job. There was no answer when he knocked on the aluminum door. He pushed his nose against a window to see if he could detect any occupants unwilling to let him inside. His reflection was suddenly bathed in outdoor shadow, and Max whipped around to find a large, imposing figure in a jaunty hat staring at him.

He was burly, with a bristling mustache. At five-foot-nine, he was only a few inches taller than Max, but his presence was towering. He took off his hat to wipe the sweat off his bald head with a handkerchief and said gruffly, in a deep voice, "What do you want, son?"

Max knew instinctively that this was a man with whom you got to your point, so he did.

"A job, sir!"

The man put his hat back on, put his gloved hands on his hips, and looked the boy over, up, and down. Max could not bear the silence. This man seemed to carry himself with great authority, almost aristocracy. Max automatically treated him like he was in charge.

"Sculpting, sir! Your mountain!" Max pointed at the flat side of the prehistoric turtle that was being covered with ropes and wood.

The man moved forward, brushing by the lad. "We won't be sculpting for another year, boy. Anyway, I don't have time for this right now!" He opened the door to the shed and went inside. In a do-or-die move that surprised even Max, he caught the door and followed the man inside.

When the man had seated himself behind a desk and began rummaging through a pile of papers, Max opened the heaviest of his two suitcases and began placing his animal creations on the desk, one by one.

The man did not even look up from the paper he was reading.

He seemed to see right through it—clearly able to condemn the little bears, swans, and ducks with one indictment. "These are trivial. I have no use for trinket-makers on my mountain."

Max stood his ground. "I am the carver of the Jefferson Park Memorial."

The man looked up from his paper. Perhaps by sheer coincidence, or by virtue of his obsession with knowing all of the nation's sculpting feats, large and small, the man's face registered a glint of recognition of the work. "The Campau, McCoy statue?"

"The same, sir!" Max answered proudly.

"Not bad . . . for an amateur . . . a novice."

Max was not sure how the next sentence escaped from his mouth; perhaps a breath of his soul sought release in the form of words. He straightened his back, his body snapping to attention in honor of what was then voiced,

"It is not novice work, sir, I assure you. I will carve a mountainside, either this one or another. Am I hired?"

The man looked up, his mustache twitching under his piercing eyes, as if it were deciding for itself whether or not to throw the switch on the rest of the face's renowned outbursts of anger and fury.

Max stood stock still, sweating from head to toe from every available pore.

The man looked back down at the paper in his hand. Silence. Max stayed at attention. Tight as a drum. The man put down the paper and got up from the desk.

"I could use some help. You're hired. I'll put you in touch with our lead foreman."

Max was taken off guard with elation. "Isn't that you, sir?"

The man actually smiled slightly. "No, son."

After all of his self-study, Max could not believe his stupidity at not recognizing the stocky stranger under the dirt, sweat, and grime. "Uh, you're Gutzon Borglum, aren't you?"

The man turned, nodded, and was out the door of the shed. With one arm, Max swept his rock résumés back into his suitcase and in seconds was following behind the famous sculptor.

"Twelve years?" Max said to the co-worker on the platform next to him. "This is going to take twelve years?" They were working on the top of Robert E. Lee's head, one of seven figures on horseback that would eventually be accompanied by an army of thousands!

"That's how long the Association is giving Mr. Borglum to finish . . . wake up from his dream!" was the worker's rather tart response.

"Have you seen the renderings?" Max asked the co-worker that night.

"Of course." Off-site, the co-worker was very patient with Max's questions. They had just finished a hard afternoon of clearing debris and were lying on their bunk beds in exhaustion. Richard Albright had been hired a few days prior to Max, and they had become fast friends. They had much in common, not the least of which was a love for sculpting and the arts in general. They were about the same age, both Yankees (Richard was from Minnesota), surrounded by southern Rebels anxious to help carve on the mountainside a lasting tribute to their civil warlords. During the next few weeks, they established a stable comradeship, both on and off the mighty mountain.

But one evening in downtown Atlanta, a stress point was revealed when Max sought the company of a young Southern belle he had met in a local bar. The Stellar God of Max's Catholic upbringing had not taken root, and Max sought to ease the tension of hanging over a cliff all day with the promiscuity offered by night with these intriguing females and their fluttering eyelashes, beguiling accents, and, most importantly, their willingness.

At first he had dabbled in incidental voyeurism, which seemed to satisfy all too briefly. It was not long before this metastasized into Hell-bent, offending eyes, hands and feet, and he was bedding and deflowering scores of pert young women without pretense, without second thoughts, without a care in the world.

The only snag in his leisure activity came from the inactivity of Richard Albright. He was a reliable worker, a good friend, and great listener, but there was a downside.

Richard Albright was a Christian. Untrammeled by the things of this world.

Max did not recognize this divine encounter either coming or going.

When Max and the other ribald co-workers compared scatological notes on what they could remember of their trysts from the night before, Richard would quietly disengage from their bawdy, bacchanalian revelry and continue chiseling, working on a platform all by himself. The other workers saw this as an affront and came to heckle him, good-naturedly at first ("Hey, Albright's not too bright after all!"), and then more and more trenchant, talking about "King Richard and his Holy Crusade," frequently behind his back. But Max's brotherly alliance with Richard Albright made him more curious than offended. How could this fine young sculptor stand up to such ridicule and derision?

Of course, much was fueled by Richard himself. Covered in dust and sweat working on the mountainside, he would constantly make symbolic "Potter-and-the-Clay" references to the granite they were taming, quoting and singing versions of the Jeremiah passage with what his co-workers would say was frequent, obnoxious fanaticism. One fellow wiseacre (the very one who, when the boss wasn't around, would cast provocative, giant shadows up on the face of the mountain by standing in front of the projection machine Mr. Borglum had devised to throw a full-scale lighted tableau tracing his Civil War portraiture directly upon the area to be carved), with some ancillary boyhood memories from his church in Indiana, said that there were days he wished Richard Albright would hide his face "in the cleft of the rock . . . and stay there!"

Richard attended the Peachtree Chapel in Atlanta every Sunday, while the other workers were sleeping off their oat-sowing from the night before. He was the only white boy in a sea of black. "Why don't you just go to the Garden Creek Baptist Church, Richard?" Max asked him one Sunday morning when Richard was quietly leaving their bunkhouse amidst a cacophony of hangover snoring.

"It's much closer than the Peachtree Chapel." This was true. The Garden Creek Baptist Church, established in 1897, was on the bank of the East prong of the Roaring River, very near the worksite. But Richard said that he preferred The Peachtree Chapel, right in the center of downtown Atlanta. Not only was it a further distance, but the congregation did not even have a building in which to meet. They met in a large white tent in an open field. "It was as if Elmer Gantry had come blazing into Atlanta," Max would say years later, toward the end of his life.

Whether it was curiosity or conviction, or a gnawing combination of both, Max was finally convinced by his buddy Richard to get out of bed one Sunday morning and come visit the Peachtree Chapel. Since arriving in Atlanta, Max had much for which to ask forgiveness, from as recently as his roll in the hay five hours previous. And his smidgeon of childhood Catholicism had thrown him a rope; all you need is a priest, a confession booth, and to do some penance, and you're on your way, fresh, clean, and free from sin. All gussied-up and ready for your next big mistake.

The Peachtree Chapel, however, was not at all similar to the St. Benedict's Cathedral in Grand Rapids, Michigan. The stately brownstone building with its steeple, parapets, and minarets was replaced by a white tent that billowed and flapped, not from any southern breezes, but rather from the bouncing, effusive congregation, all swept up in a rollicking, frothing frenzy by the music of the choir. All seven Ringling Brothers, P.T. Barnum, and James A. Bailey would have been very proud of what was happening under this particular big top. Monotonous chants and droning repetitions echoing in lofty chambers were a distant memory as Max, surprised by the unleashed behavior of these swaying, charismatic Christians, looked around him at a pulse-pounding sea of chaos. These were ebullient black folks who were giddy with welcoming intentions toward Richard and Max. Max wondered if they would have been so kind to them had they known that their boss, Mr. Borglum, was an active member of the Ku Klux Klan!

Even though Richard Albright was a staunch Baptist (like Max's statue of Isaac McCoy), he was highly attracted to this new and boisterous exposition of faith. He had hoped that this experience might stimulate his friend Max Stellar into an encounter with Jesus. But Richard realized that Max was sitting uncomfortably in his seat. He wasn't convicted. He was confounded.

It was all Max could do to stay in that seat when the large and ominous Rev. Gabriel Forsche, who had a great sense of theater, came up to the podium. He roared while standing on his tiptoes with amazing agility, intoning the congregation with ardor to "stoke up their prayer language!"

Richard and Max looked around them while hands shot up into the air, eyes closed shut, and wagging tongues of gushing glossolalia burst into the air, with the nearest interpreter clear on the other side of the Mason-Dixon line!

"They've not done this before—honestly—in all the times I've been here," offered Richard to a pale Max. Richard looked around him, wondering if these were the same "tongues" that ol' "Camel Knees"—the Apostle James—said were like rudders on a ship. If so, this Pentecostal armada was spinning wildly in circles and ramming into one another!

Both Max and Richard were relieved when Rev. Forsche put both black hands in the air to apparently douse the flaming tongues of fire, and opened his Bible, beginning the more familiar practice of sermonizing.

Richard still had high hopes that Max would meet God here at the Peachtree Chapel. He himself had always been exhilarated and never bored while listening to the electrifying sermons of the envelope-pushing, unorthodox Rev. Forsche. He was, however, unprepared for the idea that Max had already dragged God into a strange bedroom the night before, and that He was now going to use Gabriel Forsche to make it public!

"Shittim Shish ke-bab" was the sermon title, and Rev. Forsche dove right into Numbers, Chapter 25. As the story goes, Israelite men are goin' pagan by indulging in sexual immorality with Moabite women. God gets hoppin' mad. He tells Moses to wipe 'em all out! Kill all 24,000 of the fornicators! (AMEN!) While all the killin' is goin' on, some cocksure Israelite *inamorato* by the name of Zimri decides to shack up with some Midianite princess—what was her name? Oh, yes, Cozbi!, Well, they both go a-struttin' into the tent to tend to business—sassy as jay birds. (HALLELUJAH!) They walk right underneath the big, long priestly nose of Phinehas, the grandson of Moses's brother, Aaron. Well, sir, Phinehas grabs himself a big, long priestly spear—the ones used for stickin' unclean pigs with, and follows them into the tent, walkin' slow enough to give 'em just enough time to get "preoccupied" (PREACH IT, BROTHER!). While they're a-goin' at it, Phinehas raises that there spear above the couple, bouncin' like a couple o' fish on a hot skillet, and jams it straight through both of them, all the way into the dirt below. Yes, sir—Phinehas gave a whole new meaning to the "Tent of Meeting" that day! (PRAISE THE LORD!) They sure 'nuff met God—pinned to the ground, squirmin' an' all embarrassed like in their birthday suits! God don't take kindly to those that try and pick wedlocks. 24,002 were skewered that day! (AMEN!)

"And all I have left to say about that there strumpet Cozbi is—" He paused, casting for an echo, alerting his audience—agog with anticipation—that their cue was at hand.

"—drink dirt! (DRINK DIRT! DRINK DIRT!) A whole lot of death could have been avoided if, beforehand, that trollop from Midian had imbibed on Israel's priestly potion of a fifth of Numbers on the rocks—a mixed drink of holy water and tabernacle dust. (DRINK DIRT! DRINK DIRT!) The only prescribed bitter water that can supernaturally flush out fleshly, adulterous whims, fancies, and secret histories! Down the hatch, hussy! (DOWN THE HATCH! DOWN THE HATCH!) Only then can we allay any jealous suspicions about premeditated unfaithfulness. After bellying up to the bar, either she's doubled over, her guilty innards all fired up with a curse, or she innocently wipes her smiling mouth and says, 'Cheers!' (CHEERS! CHEERS!)

"Sadly, she ended up raising her glass to something much harder to swallow. And it sure 'nuff wasn't livin' water—that vast, everlasting aquifer that Jesus offered to the woman at that pitiful Samaritan well! (HALLELUJAH!)

"Ladies and gents, be careful what you're a-thirstin' for!"

Richard knew that Rev. Forsche's homiletic words were no mere coincidence and had found a home in the heart and mind of his friend, Max Stellar. However, sometimes the

Spirit's arrow can be such an accurate bullseye of blame that it completely misses the mark of repentance by insulting the host, who pulls it out with disgust. For whatever reason, the sermon that should have had the suction of conviction instead had the blast of repulsion. Max was more turned off than ever. How could a loving God initiate such wanton killing, even of the not-so-innocent? This did not seem to be an appropriate time for Richard to explain the self-imposed precepts of a holy God to Maximillian Stellar. He waited a few weeks before he broached the subject with his friend late one night in the bunkhouse. Max was ready for him and let loose on him the minute Richard tried to explain,

"How could your God allow wars?"

"How could He let innocent children die?"

"What about all the famine and disease in the world?"

"Where do you get off thinking you have the only possible way to heaven?"

Richard first apologized for Rev. Forsche's rather grisly sermon, which had indicted Max's nighttime recreation with the opposite sex on the spot.

"God just might be trying to get your attention, Max."

"Oh, really?" Max answered with the sinister sneer of the guilty and offended.

"He loves you, and so does His Son. He even . . ."

"Give it a rest, Richard!" Max was fed up with the sanctimonious excuses Richard made up in such blind absolution for his troubling God.

Richard tried another approach: admission without explanation. "I know bad things happen to good people all of the time, and there is no way to figure out why. God sometimes answers us in a way we do not like. Sometimes even tragically, from our perspective. That does not mean He does not love us and doesn't want to strike up a relationship, Max."

"I'll pass." Max folded his arms while lying on the top bunk.

Richard leaned out from his bottom bunk.

"Ever heard of the Hound of Heaven, Max? God is pursuing you. He wants to save you. He has a higher calling for you. Who do you think gave you all of your talent? He . . ."

"If that Hound of Heaven ever comes near me, so help me, I'll kick that mangy mutt to Hell and back!" Max had leaned over the edge of his bed and was looking straight down at Richard, talking much louder than necessary.

Richard ignored Max's untoward attitude, relentlessly pursuing his friend.

"Ya know, Max, Jesus stands at the door of your heart and knocks." At this, Richard took his fist and rapped the wood frame of the bunk bed underneath Max, right where his chest would be.

Max was not impressed by what he thought was an obnoxious addition to an already tedious and uncomfortable conversation.

"If you let Him in, though, He's not just coming in for tea. He will clean house in your life! He'll get rid of all the junk in your secret closets. But he'll also throw away all of the outdated furniture and tacky bric-a-brac that you have held onto over the years."

Richard could hear Max's impatient sigh above him as he lay back down, the top bunk creaking and groaning under his shifting weight.

"Not only that, He will completely remodel the place if necessary. You know, take up the old stained and smelly carpets and even knock down a wall or two!"

With that, from his bottom bunk, Richard pulled his knees up to his chin for leverage and began playfully trying to ease the pressure of proselytizing by kicking his feet under Max's bed as if Jesus himself were ripping up the floorboards right underneath him.

"Hey, shut up over there!" came an irritated voice from the far side of the hot and humid bunkhouse. It was joined by others, "Tell your Jesus friend to pipe down and go to sleep!"

"He may not know it, but we have an early day tomorrow!"

"And I'm not gonna fall off that mountain from lack of sleep!"

Max had rolled over. Richard dropped his legs, considering the subject dropped indefinitely as well. But he could not help whispering one last time up to the bunk above him, "Life with Him is a grand adventure, Max!"

Their time together on the mountain grew sporadic as Max spent more and more time down in the office, going over rendering revisions, schedules, and grant allocations from the Confederate Monument Association. Max, like the biblical Joseph, was being promoted quickly on the Stone Mountain project. This was becoming more and more obvious to everyone. And everyone, like with Joseph, was becoming more and more jealous—and envious. Gutzon Borglum had taken a liking to "young Mr. Stellar," as he called him. What's worse, Mr. Borglum taught "young Mr. Stellar" everything he knew about the art and science of sculpting on such a grand scale as Stone Mountain. He even included his scathing criticisms of other famous sculptors and their works. Like Daniel Chester French and his contemptible "seated Lincoln" for the Memorial in Washington, DC. Gutzon bragged to Max that *he,* in fact, had carved a much better seated Lincoln and that *it* should be the one going into that abominable Greek temple over there in Potomac Park.

As the months wore on, Borglum was onsite less and less, (which was a relief from his rather draconian management style). He seemed preoccupied with more pressing matters. It was as if he grew bored with the project, or frustrated with all of the bureaucracy, which was heating up. As a result, the Stone Mountain project was languishing with only the partial face of Robert E. Lee to show for all of the effort.

Finally, after nearly two years of lackluster living in Atlanta, a somewhat disillusioned Max Stellar decided to call it quits on the Stone Mountain Memorial and move to Hollywood, California. Max had seen D.W. Griffith's "Birth of a Nation" back in 1915, when he was 26, and the phenomenon of moving pictures had always stuck with him.

So, in the Fall of 1919, he boarded a train headed west. Tinsel Town of the 1920s was bustling with silent-movie production. Stars were being created seemingly overnight, all of whom required a lavish place to live. In what would amount to a complete "I told you so" from his father, Max put away his chisels and did an about-face, landing a job with an architectural firm that was building and remodeling homes for the Hollywood elite. Over the next year, Max lent his decorous vision to the estates of Lon Chaney, Gloria Swanson, Stan Laurel, Charlie Chaplin, and Mary Pickford, elevating sublimated habitats from bland and banal to exotic and exquisite. As he hobnobbed with these rich and famous clients, his connections in "the business" became more and more advantageous. It was just such a connection that would change his life. An executive at Paramount Pictures invited Max to the gala premier of a brand-new silent picture staring a charismatic matinee idol and sex symbol, Rudolph Valentino. Max sat mesmerized as the lithe and graceful movie star, who gazed at his harem of heroines with a seductive blend of passion and melancholy, swooned the females in the audience and garnered cheers from the males who wanted so badly to take his star-studded place as "The Sheik."

For the next few months, the film never fully left Max's thoughts. He could not get the handsome Arab or his romantic exploits out of his mind. There seemed to be curious parallels between the forbidden eroticism on the screen and Max's own private dalliances. Finally, as if to relieve his own mental obsession, 32-year-old Max Stellar hit upon a gutsy and outrageous idea, the perfect confluence of his two careers. As a result, he immediately set out on a hunt for just the right property. After weeks of searching, he came across the perfect face of granite rock that uniquely jutted out of a Sierra Nevada mountain range spur as it cupped its borders around a little municipality known as Vista Pacifica, some 25 miles to the east of Hollywood. With his growing fortunes from interior and exterior home designs, he plunked down the necessary funds with which to purchase 15 to 20 seemingly useless vertical acres of mountainside at the top of one of Vista Pacifica's most scenic plateaus.

With his vast and varied connections in entertainment, commerce, and real estate humming, Max was granted the permits and permission from the Vista Pacifica City Council after submitting only crude renderings of his preposterous idea (and only after they were made fully aware that he had been the right-hand man for the famous Gutzon Borglum and his Stone Mountain Memorial project). With the necessary papers in hand, Max moved to Vista Pacifica, renting office space at the bottom of the hill. Max would take "The Funicular" cable car up the main street to the base of the mountain and hike all around his property, making new sketches and corrections to old ones. He spent the evenings wiring and writing friends and colleagues near and far. He insisted on gathering the best of the best to fulfill his dream: Fellow architects from Hollywood, engineers from Los Angeles, and sculptors from across the country. One in particular was sought after under the pretext that the project would not go forward without him as lead foreman—Max's old bunkmate from Atlanta, Georgia, Richard Albright. Richard had remained in Atlanta. He was now married to his lovely wife Millicent, and they had a one-year-old son, Cody. As the Stone Mountain project was still slow going under the cumbersome weight of Georgia politicians and bureaucrats pitted against an increasingly disinterested and truant Gutzon Borglum, Richard heartily agreed to move his young family out to California to help Max carve a 100-foot likeness of Rudolph Valentino from the movie *The Sheik* onto the mountainside. As the Albright family funds were diminishing and prospects for the future growing more dismal every day in Atlanta, Richard decried that Max's invitation was the welcome "call of God" to a better future. Max dismissed this interpretation of circumstances and would not ever consider himself that sort of Providential instrument in Richard's life.

After a year of personnel gathering and detailed planning, on September 3, 1922, rumbling could be heard from miles around as the non-Rudolph Valentino sections were blasted off the Vista Pacifica mountainside. Unanimous among Max's wise circle of experts was the opinion that the carving should move in a left-to-right direction. This was due to the slope of the sheer cliff, the downhill pattern of the massive amounts of falling chiseled debris, and the flow of rainwater and its resultant erosion of growth and top soils during inclement weather.

It was not long before the project was gathering a whole host of onlookers to the site.

Many dignitaries and Hollywood celebrities came out to see the beginnings of the left side of Rudolph Valentino. The "Latin Lover" himself actually tore himself away from playing a bullfighter in the *Blood and Sand* of a Hollywood backlot to make the trip out to Vista Pacifica to view his likeness in the largest stone mirror the lusty sex symbol would ever gaze into. Max's mother, father, and sister made a special trip out to California from Michigan to see how far he had come from the little stone animals on his bedroom shelf. The mountain was a tangle of ropes, cables, and scaffolding, suspended and erected from top to bottom, making the white cliff face look as if it had run into an enormous cobweb. Rickety stairs were appearing in makeshift fashion up and down the accessible and not-so-accessible routes around the bottom half of the monstrous, unflappable granite.

After three years, "The Sheik" was right on schedule, with Max able to adequately tap dance between the stars' homes in Hollywood—which he was committed to improve—and the hillside in Vista Pacifica, which he was committed to enshrine. The little town below was growing proportionately as well. Businesses were setting up shop. Homes and schools were being built. The City Council had its hands full with this population explosion and was diligent to make sure that all construction blended with the Victorian City Hall. "The Funicular" never stopped taking the curious up the hillside for a firsthand look at Max Stellar's outrageous dream.

One night, Max received a cryptic communique from a voice from his past. It was from Gutzon Borglum, who invited him, or, who actually gruffly *ordered* him to report to a rock outcropping in the heart of the Sioux Nation in the Black Hills of South Dakota. Max could do nothing but say yes to his old boss, but with the full disclosure that he was completely committed to his Vista Pacifica project and would come only for a visit and to hear what was on Mr. Borglum's mind.

So in the Summer of 1925, Max Stellar left his friend Richard Albright in charge of "The Sheik," and took the train to *another* town named after churning waters, although not so "grand" as his own hometown in Michigan, Rapid City, South Dakota.

Fifty-nine year-old Gutzon met him at the train station and drove him immediately to Harney Peak—a 500-foot knot of ungainly granite. Gutzon was closed-mouthed about the project, and merely engaged Max in reminiscences and idle chitchat until they had hiked to the top of the crow's nest summit of Mount Harney. It was soon disclosed that Gutzon had really big ideas this time. Even bigger than the relief Civil War portrait at the now-abandoned Stone Mountain. In Harney Peak, Gutzon would carve four 60-foot heads in the round, 3/4 depictions of George Washington, Thomas Jefferson, Abraham Lincoln, and Theodore Roosevelt—a "Shrine to Democracy." (Max would later find out his old boss had been kicked off the Stone Mountain project for many suspicious reasons that Max could not authenticate. The project would eventually be handed over to another sculptor, Augustus Lukeman, and scaled back dramatically—now with only three figures on horseback. And it would not be completed for another 42 years!)

Max was more than intrigued. He made a few notes and thanked Gutzon for inviting him and asking him to be a foreman on the project, along with some 360 other dedicated men. But he had to refuse, as he was already fully committed to "The Sheik." On the train back to California, Max decided to open wide the curtain on his Rudolph Valentino. The mountain could support his stretching the side views of his rock canvas so that his project, too, would be "in the round," and his project would be a good 40 feet taller than Gutzon's presidential heads. He smiled at the thought of besting his boss in the size department. (He was also beating him in the timeline department as Mount Rushmore's George Washington head would not be completed or dedicated until July 4, 1930. However, *both* projects would remain incomplete; Borglum's four heads from the neck down, and Stellar's missing right half of Rudolph Valentino's face). In spite of his caustic personality and strong opinions, Max Stellar had liked and appreciated all that Mr. Borglum had done for him. As he waved goodbye from the Pullman car window, it never occurred to Max that he would not see Gutzon Borglum again. Ironically, in his later years, the creator of Mount Rushmore would end up living in the West and actually be buried in Forest Lawn, Glendale, only a few miles from his protégé's Rudolph Valentino dream.

Upon arriving back in Vista Pacifica, Max was astounded at how much the town had grown even in just the short time he was gone. The property at the base of the mountain had now been purchased privately, and the land was being cleared for a brand-new church. Soon construction on the church was in full force as the area was graded, and concrete foundations were poured. What with the new church at the base, and the left side of "The Sheik" now recognizable, the mountain behind Vista Pacifica was a beehive of activity.

Max's crew agreed that the three-quarter view was feasible, and blasting and sculpting commenced to reveal more of the left side of "The Sheik's" head. Richard Albright was doing a remarkable job on coordinating the efforts. Following in Max's footsteps at Stone Mountain, most of Richard's time was now spent in the office at the base. But he still liked to get up on the cliff from time to time to chisel a notch or two, or help smooth out areas by the process of "honeycombing."

On an even more rare occasion, both Max and Richard, like competing college chums, would relive the good ol' days back in Georgia by going up on the face of Rudolph to see if they could both still pass muster by hanging over the cliff to work on further expanding to the right the face of the movie star. Max very much enjoyed the company of Richard and his family. However, he grew quite irritated by the constant excitement Richard showed for the new church going up right below Rudolph's chin. One particularly busy afternoon, Richard had made an offhand comment about the new house of God, which was rumored to be called "Our Father's Evangelical Church." Max hit him hard on the shoulder and blasted Richard with as much explosive religious condescension liberally peppered with profanity as Max could think of in the heat of the moment. His voice could be heard outside the office bungalow, echoing off the rocks above and down the street for many blocks. Workers turned to each other with awkward, uncomfortable looks. They were always delighted when these two old friends—their bosses—were sportive on the mountainside, but their dismay was commensurate when one, which always seemed to be Max, went at the other's throat. Richard left the bungalow with Max still screaming at him from the doorway to "take his religion and . . ."

Max would forever regret every word and would never have a chance to apologize.

Two days later, after so much use and careless inspection, a belay line snapped while Richard Albright was "honeycombing" the forehead of Rudolph Valentino. (This smoothing process had been unnecessary—the forehead was quite smooth enough. But Richard had wanted to get as far away from the boss's bungalow as possible and occupy himself high up on the face, in solitude.) There were many screams and crashes as Richard hit planking and platforms below him in a desperate attempt to grab something, which the speed of his fall forbade. Co-workers tried unsuccessfully to grab the falling body from their own precarious, rope-dangling positions. Richard Albright fell from a height of more than 100 feet, crushing his body upon impact at the bottom and laying it out in a hideously disjointed heap. Max came rushing out of the office and ran up the hillside, where the crowd had already gathered around the body. He pushed them aside to find his worst fears of unfinished business splayed out in front of him. He burst into tears and ran back down the mountain. He did not need to wait for the coroner's pronouncement an hour later. He had already seen the truth with his own eyes. Richard Albright was dead.

Max Stellar was not seen or heard from for days. Work on Rudolph Valentino was halted indefinitely while respects were paid and every rope, cable, belay, platform, and stair was thoroughly inspected.

By family request, Richard's body was going to be taken back to the family cemetery in Minnesota. A memorial service at the base of the mountain was held in Richard's honor. A friend-of-a-friend minister (with a rather bristly, impersonal "bedside manner" and broad-stroke public speechifying that felt somewhat staged in spite of the profound truthfulness displayed throughout) from Hollywood was called upon to officiate the service. Rows and rows of chairs were set up on the cement foundation that was to be Our Father's Evangelical Church, the understandably stunned and downcast Millicent and Cody Albright sitting with their heads bowed in the front row. Next to the podium on a tripod was a large wreath of red and white flowers with a picture of smiling, joyful Richard Albright in the center. Tied to the top of the wreath was a red bow with a glitter inscription running down the ribbons,

"No good thing will He withhold from them that walk uprightly."

Before the service, the somber silence was broken by hushed murmurs and head-turning toward the back row of chairs. Max Stellar was slouching uncomfortably in the very back row, arms folded. His unshaven face was glazed with grief, transfixed with questions of sorrow. He acknowledged no one. But he soaked in the service as if filtering in all of the sensations in a desperate search for sensibility.

After a short song and a lengthy prayer, Ford Atkins approached the podium and began his requiem rhetoric, trying to capture the essence of Richard Albright without ever having met him.

"People say that God knows all about dealing with loss. After all, He sent His only Son to die for all humanity. And while that may be true, He got Him back 43 days later! Our dear departed brother Albright has left his young family and friends behind for the rest of their natural lives. We are the ones stuck here on Earth missing our husband, our father, our good friend—with no end in sight.

"The good news is that those last 43 days were more than just a cast party after the show. It was proof positive that there is something more to this life, and after. Richard Albright is there right now. One day, all of us will be able to experience the popping in and out of rooms and walking through walls that Jesus did. But, more importantly, we'll all be doing it together! We are guaranteed a reunion of family and friends all laughing and hugging and flexing the muscles of their glorified bodies! But no matter how crazy the party becomes, we will always nod in loving recognition toward Jesus as the only reason we are even there together and be thankful that we had the good sense to recognize Him while we were in this previous life. He gives a whole new meaning to the phrase 'life of the party.' Richard Albright knew all about that life and tried to share it with everyone he met. And right now, he's up there helping to write out the place cards for the wedding feast of the Lamb!"

It was here that Rev. Atkins invited volunteers (whose names Richard would be writing?) to approach the podium and say a few words about Richard. As a cool, light morning breeze sought to soothe the sorrow of those seated at the base of the mountain, heartfelt testimonies were offered from family, friends, and co-worker after co-worker after co-worker. (The only co-worker not in the long line to approach the podium was the mastermind behind the Rudolph Valentino project himself, who had brought them all together in the first place. He was sitting even lower in his seat in the back row, head down, numbly staring at his toes.) Some spoke of conversions to newfound faith they attributed to—and had made known to—Richard Albright, while others confessed of transacting their decisions later in secret, unbeknownst to the late seed-planter. Many of these speakers that morning would become part of the charter membership of the very church soon to be constructed beneath their feet—something that Rev. Atkins foreshadowed in his closing remarks.

"A local phoenix has risen from the ashes here. Jesus told the biggest loudmouth in His discipleship group that He was going to stack convert after convert upon his fisherman shoulders. The growing numbers would always be His property, but Petros was the only plenipotentiary given the contract to use wisely the rented space. We have seen right here on this property this morning that the provisions of that contract drawn up nearly 1,900 years ago, are very much alive and well—no matter what the circumstances. So long as its subsistence is the triune power of the Godhead, the force of the church is relentless. Like the prow of a ship in the tempest, nothing can stop it. Not only would Petros the earthly founder be proud today, but dear Brother Albright must have heard an enthusiastic 'Well done!' from his Savior by now!"

The service concluded with the participants singing "Rock of Ages." Max Stellar quietly disappeared. He did not even go up to console Millicent or little Cody. He spent his time in seclusion, carefully avoiding encounters with people. He spent countless hours deep in thought, brooding. Thinking back on his own life; his destiny, his family back in Michigan and their God who did not make sense, the statue in Jefferson Park, Stone Mountain, and his first meeting Richard Albright, their conversations, and Max's profound irritation with Richard's religion. Then thoughtful words from Michelangelo flashed across his brain,

"A beautiful thing never gives so much pain
as does failing to hear and see it."

In this, he avowed, for the sake of the friend whom he sorely missed, he would not fail.

After a few weeks, he appeared in public and was spotted once again overseeing his 100-foot brainchild. Whether for diversion or fulfillment none could tell, but he attacked the mountainside with a renewed vigor fueled by an unseen motivation.

By the final months of 1926, the head of Rudolph Valentino was halfway complete, and rumors were swirling that the Vista Pacifica City Council had unanimously voted to rename the town "Monument," in honor of Max's achievement.

Max was rejuvenated by this vote of confidence on behalf of the City he now called home. One day during a lunch break, Max sought solitude, a common sight among the workmen since the death of Richard Albright, and strayed over to the construction site of Our Father's Evangelical Church.

He was walking among the pallets of thousands of stacked bricks and a maze of cinder blocks that marked the perpendicular outlines of the foundation with its concrete ridges. He was so deep in thought that he did not notice the lady only a few years younger than him standing behind him. She had recognized him immediately as the resident celebrity of the town and the reason for its new name. He, on the other hand, had no idea as to the identity of this tall, blond girl. But he forced a smile, and instead of asking the reason behind her present whereabouts, he said, "It's going to be quite the church, isn't it?" The young lady put her hands behind her back in a confident, military "at ease" position, and nodded her head up to the chin of "The Sheik."

"Mr. Stellar, that is a very big rock you are carving!"

"Yes, Miss, it certainly is that." Max eyed her curiously. He suddenly grew anxious to say goodbye and get back to work. He made a move in that direction, politely saying as he passed her, "If you'll excuse me, I have to get back to work." He had gained only a few yards with his back to the lady when he heard her say,

"You know, the real rock will be *here,* where I am standing." Max turned around and looked back at the foolish blond girl, standing in the middle of the hard, gray, cement foundation.

"Who are you?" he asked, not so courteously.

"My name is Doris, sir."

"Listen . . . Doris," Max began, philosophically wearing the hard hat of a construction foreman leading a group of novices on an informative tour.

"I have surveyed this entire area, and there may be a shelf of bedrock at the base of this mountain, but it is insignificant compared to this exposed wall of granite that was just asking for someone to put a face on it!" He was sharper to the young lady than intended, as if he had to defend his position or something.

"You don't understand," replied the lady. "I'm talking about the real Rock."

Now Max grew perturbed. "Honey, this sculpture will last forever! If you will excuse me, I need to get back up there!" and he pointed to the top of the cliff while increasing his pace.

He nearly stopped dead in his tracks when Doris yelled from behind him,

"YOU'RE SURE SPENDING A LOT OF TIME AND ENERGY ON THE WRONG ROCK!"

1927. The State of California had agreed to adopt the name change of the former town of "Vista Pacifica" to "Monument," and it was thus officially recorded. A civic celebration was held at the base of the half-finished "Monument" to honor the pronouncement. Max mingled with the crowd before and after the ceremony, shaking hands and posing for publicity photos. He now lived for moments like these, as they momentarily distracted him from all of the wrong decisions in his life as well as all that he might have missed: The narcotic of narcissism was successfully numbing the aberrations of his pain and clouding his search for the hope that was in the late Richard Albright.

He spied one chubby little boy in a red-and-white striped shirt with a camera hanging by a leather strap from his neck, who was gawking at him, star-struck. Max decided to make the boy's day. Ignoring all other pleas for autographs and photos, Max walked right up to the boy and put out his hand.

"Hello, son. I'm Max Stellar. And your name would be? . . ."

In addition to the boy's florid complexion, he was wide-eyed and tongue-tied. Only after a few moments was he able to respond to the famous sculptor from Grand Rapids, Michigan. He stammered,

"Uh, Sidney, sir. Um . . . my name is Sidney."

INTERLUDE

Maria and I pulled up to the "Monument Retirement Center: Solid Gold R & R" about 12:20 on Sunday afternoon. We were here to celebrate, albeit belatedly, Esmeralda Barrington's 91st birthday, a milestone that had clocked in earlier that week. In a disquieting role reversal, Maria had cooked up a tray of her own delicious lasagna that wafted pungently as we walked through the hallway to Esmeralda's senior-citizen-friendly studio apartment. It provided one of those nostalgic nose moments, mind-jarring occasions when a distinct smell could clearly recall the scores of times this enticing aroma had poured out of the Barrington kitchen.

After we had all crowded around her little Formica dinette table, we began to eat Maria's lasagna after Esmeralda completed the ritual of her swallowing a battery of pills placed with great organizational care in little paper cups by the on-call nurse. I had noticed with a smile as Esmeralda tipped the first cup up to her lips that on her shaking wrist dangled a silver bracelet with the letters "W.V.W.W." ("Weaker Vessel: Wanna Wrestle?"). Maria had noticed it, too, and smiled at me as well. Perhaps Esmeralda no longer realized that she was wearing the once controversial bangle. After all, she was succumbing to increasingly noticeable symptoms of early Alzheimer's disease that grew more pronounced with each passing month.

Such a sainted one as Esmeralda Barrington contracting this disease was, indeed, troublesome to me. Why would God begin to call someone home with such a slow, insidious whisper, and then, by the time the prolonged beckoning became audible, the subject's sensibilities have become so marred that they cannot possibly hear or understand it? In addition, those caring for her are also taxed to the point of their own spiritual numbness and dementia! I know all of this is one of the first classroom sessions taught on sin devastation from "Fallen World 101," but it can still rattle the trusses of your faith.

It's as if God has gone into a dusty, cluttered toy closet in His hallway in the sky and pulled out an old Milton-Bradley board game called "Walk in the Spirit" for you to play with Him. Upon opening the tattered cardboard lid (that is ripped at the corners), you find that half of the playing pieces are missing!

These days, no matter how fuzzy and forgetful Esmeralda's present was at times, her grasp of the past remained remarkably lucid.

This morning I had tried out a new synopsis about the prostitute Rahab (complete with tying my red tie to the window and hanging it out of Sunday School Room C of the Educational Christianity building). This, of course, reminded me anew of the great Sid Barrington. Not knowing how many more of these lasagna lunches with Esmeralda we would be able to enjoy together, I pressed her after our meal (of which she ate meagerly) to tell me as many details about her late husband as her powers of recall, intact for the moment, could muster.

"Sid did not say too much about his growing-up years. I could only get bits and pieces from our conversations over the years. He would only talk at length about his family on those rare occasions when he was in the mood to reminisce. Or, if a photo album happened to be out and he was thumbing through it, he might make a comment or two." Esmeralda looked around the room quizzically. "I know I brought some with me when I moved here." She got up slowly from the

table and walked with fragility over to a cedar chest of draw-
ers against a far wall. She stood there for a moment, pausing
to let the original intentions of her mind catch up with her,
and then bent down to open a bottom drawer. We sought to
help her carry, with some strain, a large photo album to the
foot of her bed, but she refused our proffered assistance. We
joined her, sitting on the bed as she opened the album's large,
yellowing pages filled with the black-and-white snapshots of
what seemed like another world.

"Here's one of Sid posing with Max Stellar in front of the
mountain." She clucked her tongue as she slowly turned the
page. "That was just before Max died."

"Now, this shot was taken on the morning of our wedding
day." She pointed to a photo of her sitting in the spacious
lap of a very young Sid Barrington; the two were laughing
hysterically.

There was a lump in my throat. I could still hear his laughter.
"That must have been around 19 and 39," she said.

"But I thought you were married around 1930?" I interjected.
To which Esmeralda gave a wily smile.

"Oh, Sid was quite a kidder. He used to exaggerate to you
kids, especially on how many years we'd been married. Although
we did date off and on for about 12 years!"

"You mean it wasn't back in . . ." I pressed.

Esmeralda put her hand over her mouth mirthfully and
snickered. So did Maria.

Esmeralda gave us a wide-eyed look, as if suddenly a window
of time flew open from the past. "You know, on our wedding
day, Sid and I were not allowed to see one another. But before
the ceremony, after I was all put together in my wedding dress."
She leaned over to Maria and whispered, "You know, Honey,

they said I looked like a little Italian princess!" She then righted herself, her posture now once again including both of us in the furtherance of her story. "Well, I was ushered into the chapel so that Sid could see me for the very first time. There he was, standing in the center of the room, looking like a large, stuffed penguin in his neatly pressed suit. Well, I stood there holding my bouquet, while my bridesmaids spread my wedding dress all around. And you know what he did? He looked at me, spread his arms out, and asked me with a big, proud smile, "Well, how do I look?"

Maria gasped. "No!"

"Yes, indeed!" Esmeralda said with another gleeful snicker. "The joke wasn't so funny back then. But I never let him forget it all the years we were married! He was sure quite a character!"

She then pointed to another photograph that had caught her eye. "Here's one of Sid's family home in Monument." It was a photo taken from a distance, depicting a beautiful Victorian two-story home with a porch wrapping around three sides. There was a swing to the left side of the front door.

"I remember that porch had a beautiful view of the mountain," she said. "It could be very romantic!" The corners of her smile increased in direct proportion to whatever she was remembering. "It's sad that it had to be torn down to make room for the new freeway."

"That is quite a house!" remarked Maria.

"Oh, it was just that, Honey. There was some money in the Barrington family, you know. And not all from real estate. Um, well, *technically*."

"Oh?" Maria and I both said in unison, surprised.

"Now, knowing Sid as well as I did, I'm not sure how much of this is tall tale or not, but I think Sid and his family go as far back as Boston during the California Gold Rush in 1849. He apparently had a great grandfather—uh, Bart, I think it was—who was going to try to make it rich in the goldfields. According to Sid, he found a whole lot more than gold when he . . ."

BARRINGTON

"What is it, Obsidian?"

The whinny was not just some casual horse sigh. It was nervous. Directed. A vibration of pale, elastic lips intent on warning its owner and friend of an approaching . . . something.

Bart sat up erect. He placed his tin cup of cold coffee on a flat rock by the glowing fire. He reached over to his dusty, leather holster lying on the ground nearby and extracted his pearl-handled pistol, handed down to him from his father. The slow, menacing cocking of the gun made Obsidian whinny a second time—this time from the noise *within* the camp.

"How long have I been asleep?" Bart asked of himself and Obsidian. He had only just lain down and dozed off. Or had he? Maybe it had been hours! Hours unprotected except for the sensitivities of his trusty, light-sleeping horse. Exhausted, he. But that was no excuse for carelessness. By the look of the diminishing fire, some significant time had passed him by unconscious. Unaware. Except for Obsidian. Bart had trained his ear to nudge his subconscious whenever it heard a certain kind of whinny from his wary horse. It had saved his neck time and time again. And that time, once again, was now. There was another movement in the underbrush about 50 feet from the clearing where Bart had made his untenable, makeshift camp. He had been on his way back up to his claim-stake, which was a few more miles up the river valley. The previous few days in Hang Town had been riotous, and that had made him leery. He did not like the publicity the trial had slapped upon him. It would only lead others to inquire about the forfeited claim-stake, and perhaps they would follow him . . . .

"Bart?" came a hoarse whisper from the dark wall of spruce trees beyond the diminishing fire. Bart raised his pistol in the direction of the voice. His eye trained on the blackness. The voice apparently had a good set of eyes and ears itself and knew his quarry was coiled up like a rattler preparing to strike.

"Don't shoot, Bart! It's me, Willie!"

At the sound of the name, Bart's muscles began to relax; his pistol drooped as the taut sinews that previously held the pearl handle in a deadly vise grip began to loosen, and his held breath began to moderate. The tall, shaggy scarecrow that was Wilderness Pettit came into view.

Now that the intruder was a known commodity, Bart immediately grew angry. "I could've killed you, Willie! What in tarnation were you thinkin' comin' up on me like that in the middle of the night?"

"It's almost dawn, Bart." Well, there now was his confirmation that his dog-tired sleep had been more than a catnap! He had needed only to look up at the scudding clouds whose underbellies were aflame from the stretching and yawning eastern rays.

"They hung him. Couldn't wait till dawn, so they hung him last night. I thought I could catch up with you and tell you."

Bart swallowed, slowly. In a complete turnabout of the Prophet Isaiah's gushing sentiments about positive feedback coming from above the timberline, here were booted feet on the mountains bringing not-so-good news. But he was thinking how fortunate he had been to have cut ties with the feckless Curtis Calhoun.

They had met on the ship *Conestoga* shortly after it had departed from Boston. Bart was determined to make his fortune in the goldfields of California and get some money back to his impoverished mother. His father had died of tuberculosis some years back, leaving Bart—the instant his father took his last, labored breath—the man of the household. The combined odd jobs he and his mother found could not sufficiently make ends meet, so his mother, with great trepidation, had agreed to let Bart take an incredible, risky gamble and venture forth to find the "gold in them thar hills," as it had been so proudly reported all over the known world from some 3,000 desperate miles away.

Shipboard, Curtis had taken a liking to Bart almost immediately. Bart did not reciprocate. His mother had taught him to be a good judge of character (a lifesaver for a single mother in the rough-and-tumble Boston of 1849), and those lessons, brought to bear in the schoolroom of his mind, taught that Curtis Calhoun spelled unequivocal trouble. Apparently, the townsfolk of Hang Town had agreed with his judgment. During the harrowing nights around Cape Horn, the bobbing and weaving *Conestoga* flirted with one "Lost at sea: Down with all hands" status report after another as it made its way around the broken teeth that comprised the coastline geography of the tip of South America. Curtis Calhoun would talk brashly about all of the "drinkin' and whorin'" which would commence as soon as he returned to San Francisco from the plentiful goldfields with his bag full of riches just itchin' to be squandered. He did not mention the "Good Book" during the entire four months at sea. Bart's mother, in spite of her circumstances, had remained "God-fearin'" and told her only boy as much every time she had the opportunity. Even though he had only a distant appreciation for his mother's strong religious spine, now at sea and bunking with the likes of Curtis Calhoun, the "Good Book" of his mother provided much-needed ballast to stabilize Bart and give him discernment into this character's character.

When talk arose of their becoming partners in the gold-fields, Bart and his mother's "Good Book" raised up an army of warning red flags. Bart would give no such filial agreement to this ill-fated ruffian. However, since the overwhelming new world of frontier San Francisco threatened to engulf them, Bart and Curtis initially remained side by side whilst they gathered their wits, got their bearings and supplies, and headed for the goldfields. Only once did they temporarily part company. On the evening before their departure by stagecoach to Hang Town, Bart stayed behind in their hotel room while Curtis Calhoun drank himself into oblivion in the saloon downstairs and woke up the next morning in a call girl's bed. Upon arriving in Hang Town in 1850, the same year California became a State and was admitted into the precarious Union, the two sought the livery stable where they could purchase horses to transport themselves to the farthest reaches of the adjacent river valley to any unclaimed land on which they might prospect. Bart had immediately bonded with a huge, dark horse hobbled near the anvil, a fact not lost on the observant blacksmith. Obsidian was jet-black, with remarkably penetrating yellow eyes—deep pools of complete awareness.

"He's a loyal servant, that one!" said the blacksmith. "He's got an eye for spottin' trouble, he does." Bart patted Obsidian's sleek neck.

"You don't say," he said, never taking his eyes off the horse's, or vice-versa!

"Yup," continued the blacksmith. "If he takes a likin' to ya, he will protect you with his life. He saved mine on many an occasion."

"Really?"

"Yup."

Bart raised his dark eyebrows at the blacksmith, "Why would you be willing to sell such a protective animal?"

"'Cause I'm fixin' to leave these here parts. I'm a-going back to Sacramento. I only came up here to set up shop for the miners. Once I heard they'd discovered gold at Sutter's, I knew towns would crop up everwhere, and they'd need themselves a smithy. I've been workin' for a spell, but I miss my little shack by the Sacramento River. I need the money to get back. I'll buy me another horse later on if need be. But I'll wager there be no replacin' this here Obsidian!"

Maybe he's sellin' me a line of goods, thought Bart, but that was the extent of his bargaining power. He found himself saying "I'll take him!" unwisely early, before suspicious looks, shrewd delays, poker faces, and coy price-parrying could have knocked the deal into a more buyer-friendly arena. Perhaps the anxious, yellow-eyed look from Obsidian had won him over so thoroughly that he had thrown his purse-string caution to the California winds. As it turned out, the horse was worth every penny—solid gold, as it were. In spite of himself, the prudence of his mother and her "Good Book" had followed him around the continent.

On the other hand, impecunious Curtis Calhoun had thrown a bit too much cavorting money over the counter to the Lucky Nugget bartender and onto the silver nightstand tray of Lady Mae the night before, so he could only wrap his pocketbook around, and be saddled to, a recalcitrant sorrel nag the blacksmith was only too willing to sell cheaply. "He may not look so good," he offered to Curtis as a thin veil of empathy and encouragement, "but he'll get you to where you're goin'."

True enough. They had made their way high up the river valley with all of their gear without any incident. Curtis staked his claim first. Bart waited until he was further up the valley. He was looking for telltale signs of gold deposits just as they had been described to him by mendacious know-it-all passengers on-board the *Conestoga*, who, with practiced panache, liked to hear themselves talk. They had not amassed any wealth worthy to speak of, but they could certainly talk up quite a blustery storm on how to get it.

Before long (after going down and filing their claims officially with the clerk at the Hang Town Assay Office), picks were heard pounding against rock from both camps, and dirt was flying everywhere, the excitement of potential riches motivating every back-breaking, arm-straining arc. Even with no distinguishable signs of gold (nugget or dust), that first week was fueled by tale after passionate tale of untold millions as relayed by sailor, fellow prospector, and passerby from their long months of travel, holding both Bart and Curtis captive in its dazzling grasp.

A third prospector happened by in their second week. A man wizened by the elements (making him look much older than in actuality) but with a warm smile capable of stretching across his leathery face in spite of his grizzled features. He had a prime claim-stake just a few miles below Curtis and Bart and had decided to pay them a respectable, cordial visit.

These were times when suspicions ran high—when a man's intentions were always called into question. But it took no time at all for both Curtis and Bart to take an affectionate liking to Wilderness Pettit. Soon, many an evening was spent around one of the three campfires, singin' songs, tellin' tales, confessin' sins, and pinin' for home. Wilderness "Willie" Pettit was the consummate gold-mining professional. He had made a few thousand dollars already on his claim-stake and knew a goodly plot of mother earth when he saw it. On the night when the host campfire was in front of the Curtis Calhoun tent, Willie spoke thus about the very ground he was sitting upon.

"This could really be somethin', Curtis! I can smell it." This was given more weight by Willie's giving a full account of his winnowing-stick successes in parched distant lands.

"You keep right on diggin', you hear? Mark my words, pay dirt is on the way!"

The next morning Curtis was invigorated by Willie's prophecy and would have dug halfway to China had he not noticed that his sorry old nag had chewed clean through its hobble and was nowhere to be found!

Bart could hear him swearing clear up the canyon. He rode Obsidian down into Curtis' camp to find him kicking at the woodpile and screaming at the gods. Curtis was sure that the mother lode was inches away from his next pick swing in the gaping hole of two weeks' effort. He had to have a horse handy once his gold was discovered. How would he ever haul it all down to the Assay Office in Hang Town? Bart offered Obsidian in the Willie-blessed likely event that gold was soon to be discovered by Curtis Calhoun. While appreciative of the offer, Curtis would have none of it (much to the secret relief of Bart). He wanted this bonanza all to himself, including its transportation.

"Guard my digs, will ya, Bart?" Curtis growled while he dusted himself off, put on his frayed hat, buckled up his holster, flung his coat over his shoulders, and trudged off.

"Where're you going?" Bart called.

Curtis did not even turn around. "Hang Town. I gotta get me another horse!"

"With what?" Bart responded. He had seen Curtis hand the blacksmith his last plugged nickel for the nag. Most certainly he had no credit to speak of with the bank in town, so Bart was sure Curtis could not secure a loan. Nor was it likely that he could cull any financial assistance from among the denizens of the Lucky Nugget Saloon, or wheedle from Lady Mae and her saucy, buxom courtesans in the noisy brothel upstairs. They would not take kindly to any suggestion to melt down the gold rings dangling from their porcine snouts.

"I'll figure somethin' out. Just watch the place, will ya?" and he disappeared into the dense woods.

"Character." That was all his mother had said after she had hugged him on the crowded wharf of the Bostonian quay. She had pointed her dainty but determined finger high up (his 22 years of growth had far surpassed his mother) to the center of Bart's forehead as triplicate charge—admonition—warning, and repeated, "Character. Not only have one," she had told him, "be able to judge one." He could almost feel the press of that finger against his forehead when Curtis Calhoun had sashayed his way up to the railing of the rolling *Conestoga* and struck up a conversation with a seasick Bart Barrington. He could also picture Farmer Jesus standing there in the orchard on top of Mount Sermon, tellin' the folks to be discerning fruit inspectors.

Now, as a new day was dawning, and he heard the news from Willie, he knew he had judged rightly. The only "somethin'" that Curtis had figured out in order to procure a second horse was to steal one. That was a capital offense in 1850 Hang Town—the swift meting out of life-threatening justice giving the place its ominous name. This christening originally occurred after three ruffians were summarily hanged after robbing an old man of his $6,000 in gold, and the town's name had stuck.

There had not even been time for Bart to saddle up Obsidian and make his way down the mountain to the outdoor trial. The owner of the stolen horse identified Curtis as the very one he had caught in the night trying to take his prize filly out of his barn, and they had strung him up!

There was one wicked irony in the Hang Town justice system, however. Curtis was seated upon the very horse he had tried to steal! His hands were tied behind his back; a teardrop-shaped noose hung from a high branch in a nearby gnarled old oak tree and was tightly secured around Curtis's skinny neck.

The preacher had smelled the eternal smoke and run up to a nervous and sweating Curtis, blurting out how much of the 23rd Psalm the condemned had missed over his lifetime because of his recidivism. It was an uncaring heathen who was stationed at the hindquarters of the filly when the preacher began to intone King David's pastoral soliloquy, and he slapped her rear end with his whip, sending Curtis Calhoun straight into the jaws of Hell before the preacher could even drag the tormented soul from the valley of the shadow of death to sit beside the shore of any still waters and helplessly stare at the unattainable.

"Thanks for tellin' me, Willie. Sorry I pulled the gun on ya," was all Bart could say once Wilderness Pettit had relayed the sequence of events that was the swift hanging of Curtis Calhoun.

Character. Have one. Judge one. "Thanks, mother!" Bart sighed after Wilderness had slinked off into the woods, back to his own claim-stake.

Out of what little respect Bart could muster for his ill-fated prospecting neighbor, he had traveled weeks later back into Hang Town to see the whitewashed tomb with its merciless gravestone,

"Curtis Calhoun
1826–1850
Horse thief who rode on the Devil's knee"

and to acquire the Calhoun claim-stake. "Might as well work it for him and see if there's anything to it," Bart had surmised (collusion no longer being a risk with the late scoundrel now that he was firmly and safely planted six feet under). It was back-breaking work picking at his own plot of land, let alone alternating between two holes to nowhere! But to honor the dreams of Curtis Calhoun, Bart Barrington would make a go at both. He did not get to work on the Calhoun hole until after that first winter. It was enough for him to keep himself alive sitting on his own grubstake inside his own wickedly porous, lean-to shanty. Once the ground—and his backside—had thawed, Bart decided that the time had come to work the contiguous landfill. Standing deep within the hole Curtis had so painstakingly dug, Bart's pick slammed for a full straight week into the stubborn side of earth to his left. When the dust cloud had abated, Bart Barrington discovered that Wilderness Pettit had been right! As the California sun singled out the northeast wall in the hole, glints of gold sparkled in the soil, varicose veins not only decrying the age of the earth but also announcing the next sweepstakes winner of the grand prize in the game of life and chance.

More delicate excavation revealed golden tributaries that widened into significant, solid masses. Bart climbed out of the hole, short of breath from the exertion and the discovery, but with the presence of mind to go over to his saddle, which was slumped over a contentedly grazing Obsidian, and pull out his pistol. He set it on the rim of the hole and climbed back in. Once a discovery of this magnitude became known, any man could stoop to the lowest of behavioral levels, butchering frail frontier laws, and unhesitatingly put a bullet in the back of the owner with a cold, calculating eye, taking the spoils for himself.

Character. Have one. Judge one.

The only confidant worth risking (because of his already-proven character) was Wilderness Pettit. With enough money of his own accumulated, Wilderness helped guard the claim with his well-trained rifle, while Bart made his brush with serendipity known at the Assay Office in Hang Town. But as soon as his first leather satchel of gold was plopped down on the mahogany counter, word would seep down into the cracks of Hang Town, alerting the dregs of the mineral-laden Earth that one prospector had indeed struck it rich and would need to have his mother "load" lightened just a bit!

It was dusk when Bart was walking toward the stables to retrieve Obsidian and head back up the mountain, his gold stored securely in the Assay Office safe, and his voucher confirming as much just as safe in the inside lining of his hat. There was a zinging sound at his right ear. A foreign sensation at first, but then all-too-familiar stories told to him in Boston of the untamed West and its equally untamed lawlessness simultaneously bombarded his memory and reflexes, confirming that he was now falling headlong into the real thing. A second zing ripped off a few feet of white clapboard from the nearby church. A third shattered a stained-glass window above his head. Bart dropped down behind the stairs leading up to the church's front door, but not before a fourth shot penetrated his right thigh with an excruciating lightning bolt of pain that sent trembling shock waves from muscle and nerves torn asunder up and down that side of his body.

There was a rustling in some nearby bushes . . . and then the sounds of stealthy boots on rain-crusted gravel. *More than one predator by the sound of it!* thought Bart as he lay inert in the tall grass behind the church steps. Pain from his leg surged, causing him to wince as he pulled out his pistol in an effort to defend himself and the voucher in his hat.

As the growing sounds of tread in his direction closed in upon him, Bart, cornered between staircase and church wall, cocked his pistol and steadied it toward the approximate whereabouts of the noises in the darkness. He tightened his finger around the trigger. There was a "BANG!" from above his head. Bart painfully whipped around to see behind and above him. Both church doors had burst open, and out had come a woman screaming. She ran down the stairs and looked in both directions. Her female senses quickly declassified the whereabouts of the potential target's secret hideaway, and she bolted to her right. In moments, she was facing the barrel of Bart's pistol, once she had found him lying in the grass like a desperate, wounded animal.

She responded in kind. "Put that away!" she ordered. Bart looked at her, incredulous, and was about to lower the pistol when the woman's lacy collar was elevated from behind her neck and she was lifted high up into the air, the back of her dress in the grip of one of Bart's would-be assassins.

"Out of the way, shrew!" came a voice from behind the flailing female. She was flung in a heap in front of the church stairs.

Out of the darkness a rifle protruded, pointed at Bart's head. The motivations were made manifest with a gruff voice from under a black hat saying, "The voucher, mate. Now!"

Bart made every attempt to steady his pistol and give a show of force, but his bleeding leg was draining the fight out of him. His red pant leg and the widening puddle underneath were equally obvious to his opponent. His hat lay by his right elbow, and, helpless and defeated, he slowly made an attempt to reach for it.

"BANG!" the noise from above repeated itself. "Oh, no you don't, King!" Down the stairs flew a black vision, wraithlike, with a disheveled, white-haired contrail. He looked to be carrying a large, black box under his arm. A voice deeper than the Earth's core shook the stale night air: "King!"

The man at the other end of the rifle did not move. He only gruffly wheezed malodorously between obviously clenched teeth. "Back off, god man!" The black wraith paid him no heed. He came and stood, facing his adversary, legs spread apart, in front of Bart. From Bart's point of view on the ground, the man seemed as tall as a mountain. He was broad, too. Rugged. Tested. Intolerant. Perhaps this was one of the "descendants of Anak" according to the Old Testament stories told him by his mother back in Boston. A surviving giant in the land.

"Over my dead body, milksop!" his resonant baritone voice seethed. He deftly moved the big, black box into both of his gigantic hands with an intense vise-grip. From his line of vision below, Bart could see that it was not a big, black box after all. It was a very large book.

The tall man with a voice like thunder shoved his arms stock-straight out in front of him, hands still gripping both edges of the big, black book. The center of the book butted right up against the barrel of King's rifle.

"Fire, King!" The invitation was at once bold and daring. Ludicrous. The bullet from the rifle could easily plow through the worn pages of the book, make its sinister way right into the big man's chest, and escape to form a large smoking puncture into the white clapboard wall of the church. The white-haired obstruction was unmoved by any threat.

"I aim to!" said the sibilant voice of King, an unseen cloud of halitosis emitting from the darkness.

"Then get on with it, maggot! Come on!" the big man bellowed, further pushing back the rifle barrel with his book. "I defy you to put a hole in the Word of God!" There was silence on the other side of the rifle barrel.

"Here I raise my Ebenezer!" The white-hair flared in a light evening breeze that was now tempering the stifling, moisture-ridden air from the drizzle of that afternoon. But the large Bible held steady, still level with the rifle, rock-like.

"Father!" screamed the woman lying in the mud nearby, "Don't, please!"

"Shut up, vixen!" spat King, giving her a baleful glare.

"Fret not, child. He has sown the wind and will now reap the whirlwind," said her father, with confidence hewn from granite. His body did not even quiver as his bigger-than-life voice engulfed the area. A crowd began to gather. Not so much attracted by all of the yelling and commotion, which was commonplace in Hang Town, but by the unexpected sound of the voice coming from an unexpected side of the church on an unexpected day that was certainly not any Sunday.

"Go on, fire!" screamed the voice under the chaos of white hair. There was a threatening rustle from the nearby bushes behind King. The woman gave a gasp of panic. Her father and his book did not move. He knew this was not an ambush by King supporters—it was a retreat. The stare-down continued. It was now up to King.

"Witherin', are you? You gutless poltroon!" provoked the acid tongue with enough flame-throwing condescension to fill a universe.

King made not a sound, but the rifle barrel sank ever so slightly.

The big man leaned into his book, and yelled, "Do your will or be gone, apostate! Crawl back under that rock in the Valley of Hinnom from where you came!"

The rifle withdrew, and the craven King suddenly disappeared with a mad, cowardly scramble back into the cover of darkness.

The man towering above the now-dizzy Bart Barrington remained rigid, still holding the big, black book erect out in front of him like a shield against the unknown noises diminishing into the night.

The spell of his fixation with the "pestilential minions of darkness" was broken only by the gentle hand of his daughter upon his arm. Her face was soiled, her luxuriant hair ruffled, her dress muddy and tattered, but her gaze into her father's eyes was tranquil and reassuring. It was enough to relax the stiffened bones and tight muscles of the outrageously daring preacher.

She immediately dropped down to her knees behind him to care for the victim, who had fainted.

The addled brain of Bart Barrington awoke looking up into the face of an angel. Dazzling beauty determinedly attending rugged scruffiness with one ultimate goal in mind: his complete health and well-being. While Bart was still unconscious, the town doctor had dislodged the bullet from where it hid, inches from his festering femur. The mending could now begin.

"Is he awake?" came that voice again. According to Bart's insensate perceptions, it came from far off—from an indeterminate direction. Only the increased volume brought distinction to the garbled voice's whereabouts.

"Well, Susannah? Is he awake, I said?"

"Yes, father," spoke the angel, reassuringly, "He appears to be coming to."

Instantly there was a large Nephilim hand jutting out into Bart's blurry line of vision. When Bart failed to muster the energy to raise his unresponsive right hand in greeting, the thistle-headed banshee—with so many renegade strands of vibrating white hair shooting out in all directions that God had forgotten the number—came in for a closer look that included his revealing rows of stately teeth, all standing at attention, framed in a crescent moon smile. With his face an inquisitive, imposing distraction, he grabbed Bart's limp hand and shook it violently.

"Damascus. Please to meet you, Mr . . . ?"

Damascus? Bart's maimed powers of recall miraculously healed to seize the moment, and he was back in Boston on his mother's lap, hearing the story of Saint Paul's conversion. This gigantic, smiling face in front of Bart's, from which shooting rays of teased white follicles fanned out in all directions like the puffy head of a dandelion . . . Could it possibly be the same glorious vision that had once gripped the Apostle?

"Damascus Gulch." There was a deep vibration rippling through the bed—the man was chuckling. "Yeah, I know, I know! It sounds like a place you go to to get yer act together! Well, no matter. That's my name all right, by the order of Melchizedek!"

"Father, don't tire him. I don't think he understands." The angel had spoken, but her soothing voice had been relegated to the fuzzy outer edges of Bart's awareness.

"You can call me 'Cuss' for short. That's what all the folks call me aroun' here." The lack of comprehension on the dazed face of Bart Barrington did not seem to deter the booming dandelion—which was inching ever closer—from continuing. He was getting decidedly louder, apparently to combat the emotionless face with which he was trying to communicate. Bart squinted in an effort to rewaken his brainwaves through his rheumy vision. The dandelion was now a wide-eyed orb in front of him. Nose to nose.

"I've been called 'Cuss' since I was a boy! My momma gave me that nickname 'cause 'Damascus' took too darn long to say, I guess. So, she just lopped off the first two syllables for sheer convenience's sake. I was also a bundle o' trouble when I was a lad, accordin' to my momma—so she thought 'Cuss' best explained my miscreant behavior!" The bed shook again with his laughter. "I was an explosive personality!"

"Father, please! Let him rest."

The dandelion ignored the angel. "So 'Cuss' it has remained. 'Course, you should count your blessings, Damascus!" he said half to himself as he shook his large head reminiscently, pausing for any recognition from the head on the pillow. The blank stare in return was just enough encouragement for him to forge onward. "Well, for one thing, you wouldn't want a nickname comin' from either of the *first* two syllables of my name, now would ya?" More raucous laughter, causing mattress tidal waves. Deduction of all this would have taken some thought even for a cogent Bart Barrington. Susannah Gulch, however, who had heard this salty conjecture before, now rushed to the bedside to quell her father once and for all.

"Father, let him rest!" The insistence in her voice caused the dandelion head to recede into the distance as the lights in the room fluttered and were then snuffed out with the onset of more unconsciousness.

When Bart was well enough, he immediately hobbled over to the Livery Stable to pay for the new blacksmith's great care of Obsidian during Bart's sudden disablement and recovery.

After a few more days, he was ready to make his way back up the mountain to relieve Wilderness from the guarding of his claim-stake.

"I thought you was dead!" exclaimed Wilderness Pettit when he saw the limping Bart Barrington come into view, leading Obsidian behind him.

"I thought I was, too!" And, over a blazing campfire, Bart recounted the last week-and-a-half to Wilderness, including his deadly encounter next to the Hang Town church.

"I was this close to goin' down and checkin' up on ya," said Wilderness, with soiled thumb and forefinger pinched close together. "But I didn't dare leave this here gold mine unattended. Especially with the likes of King and his marauders lurkin' about!" Bart expressed his great appreciation for his loyal friend. He even described the smoldering clergyman, Damascus Gulch, and his beautiful daughter, Susannah.

Wilderness had seen both father and daughter around Hang Town on the rare occasions when he came into town ("That girl is mighty fetchin'," he would say after she had walked by). He heard in Bart's description and the look on his face that this girl had stolen his heart. Even Obsidian, with equine premonitions, shook his ebony head and shivered his neck muscles as the story unfolded, knowing that affections toward him were now being shared. Every new bagful of gold extracted from a generous Earth and trekked down into town gave ample opportunity for Bart to "pay a call" on Susannah Gulch. His stays in town became more and more prolonged. He bequeathed to Wilderness a healthy share of his newfound wealth for looking after the ever-widening hole in the ground. He also wired a goodly sum home to his mother in Boston.

Now renegade prospectors were surging all around the area, claiming land in a desperate effort to get their grubby hands on any trickle of the lucrative gold vein that Bart had been draining, so Wilderness was well paid from his largess for fending off any encroachers.

Bart came to appreciate and even respect the surly preacher, Damascus Gulch, and his predilection toward all things "fire and brimstone," as he sought to set ablaze and melt the spiritually bankrupt gold-rush establishment of Hang Town with the white heat of the almighty breath of God.

"His bark is worse than his bite," was always Susannah's soothing response when hackles were raised around the Sunday supper table, which Bart now regularly joined. Damascus occasionally stormed outside after an altercation arose between the volatile preacher and Bart on any number of incendiary subject matters, particularly those ignited by the Good Book. Bart's fleeting memories of his mother's simple lessons were no match for the finely tuned oracles of God that stridently exploded from the rapier tongue of Damascus Gulch. On numerous occasions, he would storm into his study and bring back the very big black book that had saved Bart's life, literally and figuratively, slam it down on the dining-room table, and open it to whatever passage would pulverize the controversy of the day.

"I believe in 'Hoof Theology'!" he had said one day, as he recklessly shoved the plates and silverware aside—clearing the way for more saber-rattling—and predictably plopped the large book down onto the table, nearly overturning the water glasses and gravy boat.

"Know what that is, Barrington?"

"No, sir."

"It comes from Exodus, Chapter 10," to which he had confidently turned. "Moses was lockin' horns with Pharaoh, see—it was pitch-black bedlam everwhere in Egypt. Pharaoh told Mo in the darkness that he finally could go—but he had to leave the livestock behind. Moses told him 'Nothin' doin'! Not a hoof will be left behind!' he said. In other words, no compromises,

Barrington! Compromisin' ain't who you should be, and it taints who you are!"

I know, I know, thought Bart, picturing his mother. Character. Have one. Judge one.

Speaking of mothers, Damascus's mother had sure named him appropriately. Every time he opened his mouth, there was blinding light—whether you had requested the illumination or not!

"You've already preached once today, father!" Susannah would say with a sigh. She always kept a sense of humor about her father, even when she was being assailed by his orations. She was a believer in the God of her father and of her beloved mother, rest her soul. Missy Gulch had died shortly after their arrival in California, following their long frontier expedition from Chicago, Illinois.

"It was the travelin' that kilt her!" Damascus boomed one Sunday afternoon after supper when Bart had reluctantly brought up the subject of Susannah's mother. "Just like Rachel, Jacob's wife."

"Now, father!" Susannah pleaded. Her delicate finger was in the proverbial dike, but the dam burst nonetheless, as it had every time her combative father was so prompted.

"Honey, you just sit tight and listen while I learn yer boy-friend somethin'."

At this surprise description of their budding relationship, Susannah quickly glanced at Bart and just as quickly looked down at her china plate to break his returned gaze. Bart noticed a blush tinting the porcelain patina of Susannah's complexion.

"It's right here in Genesis, Chapter 35!" Bart was forced to re-establish eye contact with the towering preacher at the head of the table who had, once again, retrieved his gigantic Bible, and scattered the dinnerware with it.

"Them boys Simeon and Levi, they were some characters, they were. They cooked up such a plot of revenge after their little sister Dinah was, well, taken advantage of, by that rogue stallion, Shechem. He was fixin' to marry her after the incident, to try and make things right. Too late! Simeon and Levi cunningly told Shechem's father and the whole bunch in the palace they had to go an' get circumcised in order for them to agree to give up their sister to marry. The whole city, all them ruddy 'n randy males, had to go under the knife!" Damascus went wide-eyed with this last phrase, expelling the words with a sinister whisper, and he leaned his head closer to Bart.

"Do you know what circumcision is, Barrington?"

"I think so. Yes." Now Bart was blushing.

"Well, it ain't pleasant—that's fer dang sure! A baby boy's very first nightmare, just eight days after comin' into the world."

"Father!" Susannah tried to intervene. But Damascus Gulch had very little use for interlocutors on any occasion, related or otherwise. "They say afterwards that the second and third days are the worst!" Bart cringed. He stared down at the sterling silver knife gleaming on his plate. He could feel his protective legs stiffen and cross tightly together under the dining-room table. Susannah covered her head in her hands.

"Well, there they were, all of them fightin'-age men and boys all curled up like they was back in the womb, moanin' and groanin' with searin' pain comin' directly from down yonder at the fork in the road! And you know what? Simeon and Levi knew that's exactly when they should come a-stormin' into town, killin' all the males with their swords—who had seen enough of knife blades about then!" He smiled wickedly. "They even slit the throats of the groom-to-be and his daddy." Turtle-like, Bart lowered his neck into the protective hole of his collar.

"But they didn't stop there. They looted the whole town! Cartin' off the screamin' women and children, took all the livestock, and set fire to the whole dang place!"

"Father, what does all this have to do with mother?" Susannah had heard this comparison many times before, but she was hoping her question might wrestle the story to the ground and bring it to a welcome conclusion so that the squirming Bart could relax, uncross his legs, and hold his head high again.

"I'm comin' to that, Honey!" Damascus looked down at his daughter, scowling at her impertinence but plowing ahead without any hint of closure.

"In all the smoke, God told Jacob to get out of town—fast! Other towns were sure to get wind of the sacking of Shechem and form an alliance of some sort to hunt down the murderers! His wife, Rachel, was goin' to give birth to Benjamin any time and should not be travelin', but for the sake of life and limb, Jake's family had to skedaddle, and there was Rachel, bouncin' around in the back of the wagon like a sack o' beans as the caravan made a fast getaway. She had Benjamin shortly thereafter and died during the birthin'. It was just that way with Missy. The travelin' was too much for her."

It had been a long journey, but he had finally come full circle.

Bart could not resist. "Is that why you left Chicago, Cuss?"

"Huh?" Damascus furrowed his brow and glared at Bart with suspicion. Susannah had caught on and giggled.

Bart played on. "I mean, sir, did you have to leave Chicago for the same reason that Jacob left . . . where was it? Shechem?"

The light suddenly dawned on Damascus, and he belly-laughed heartily.

"Oh! No, son!" he chuckled. "We didn't have to get out of town like that. We were law-abidin'. We came out West, peaceable

like!" Damascus liked Bart's occasional forthrightness. He also
enjoyed having someone to spar with at the supper table, week
after week, other than his wholesome, quick-to-protest-and-
politely-get-out-of the-boxing-ring daughter.

"But I'll tell you this!" he bellowed, as Susannah sighed hopelessly.

"I don't think Joseph quite got over his older brothers'
shenanigans that caused the killin' of his mother an' all. He
was probably 10 or 12 at the time. That explains why he did all
them spiteful things to his starvin' brothers when he became
Pharaoh's right-hand man."

Damascus Gulch gave the loveless clanging cymbals from
1 Corinthians 13 a whole new dimension.

Bart nodded his head in an insincere show of agreement in
order to change both the subject and focus to Susannah, who
seemed deep in her own thoughts.

Why did the God of her kind and gentle mother and the
God of her frenzied father not seem the same at all? The two
were not as one, but rather like distant cousins from opposite
sides of the tracks. Opposite upbringing. Opposite personalities.
Opposite sex. "How could this be?" Susannah would wonder.
Over the ensuing weeks, Bart usually would offer nothing to
unravel her vexation over a cross-dressing, hybrid Deity. Except
on one particular Sunday afternoon, after the front door of the
parsonage had safely slammed behind Damascus, who was apo-
plectic with rage that had resulted from another virulent supper
"discussion," he merely said to Susannah, "Maybe God's not so
different after all. Maybe it's not Him, but rather us that's different. He's just handin' out different clothing for us, depending
on our weather. You know, bigger, heavier coats for those always
in a storm, and lighter clothing for those who will be able to see
more sunshine in their lives."

Susannah brightened with a smile; she leaned over and kissed Bart for the very first time. Bart was not quite sure why. Was it for the wisdom he had so inadvertently brought to the table, which had suddenly made sense to her, or maybe just the fact that he had tried to offer anything, however stupid or poorly thought through? Regardless, he relished every second of their first kiss.

The pair were married within months, on a torrid, swelter-ing Saturday in July 1851, before a packed crowd of scorched, dehydrated, frantically fanned faces in the little Hang Town church. Stentorian Damascus Gulch presided over the wedding ceremony of his only daughter to suitor Bart Barrington. He did not merely officiate—he adjudicated over the proceedings, taking full advantage of the situation to lay out for the new couple, and everyone within earshot, just what God expects from his wayward children. His dark, black suit only accentuated the intimidation. With his uncombed white hair exploding in all directions about his head, he looked as if he had actually been present during the earth-shattering events from Genesis, Chapter Three.

"That sly ol' serpent will come in many forms, children. Don't pay him no heed, you hear?"

His searing eyes shot to his left and drilled into Bart's as he spoke thus,

"Bart, do not let Susannah out of yer sight lest she be tempted by whoever, whatever, or wherever her weaknesses are! God will come a-callin' for you in the cool of the afternoon and make you give an account for your inaction. No fig leaf is gonna save you. The Bible says it is a fearful thing to fall into the hands of the living God."

Falling into yours would be no church picnic, thought Bart.

". . . and He's especially short-fused with husbands who should know better! Even Saint Peter says that the Almighty sticks His fingers in His ears the minute one of those types tries to start talkin' to Him!"

Now that was reassuring! thought Bart as he stood stiffly in front of his future, preacher father-in-law, sweating profusely while taking this verbal punishment with his chin held high in a charade of confidence, with his back to the sun-dried audience.

Damascus Gulch then turned to his daughter.

"And you, little girl," upon which Susannah grew wide-eyed with embarrassment, leaning toward her father and whispering with a forced smile through clenched teeth, "I am 19 years old and about to be married, Father!" The preacher ignored the under-her-breath remonstrance and spoke right over his daughter's head.

"You stay away from any bad apples, you hear?" This gave cause for some chuckles in the perspiring crowd, as much to relieve the tension of Damascus Gulch and his commencement address than anything else. Susannah was not smiling. She raised her eyebrows to her father in an intense, contumacious expression of *Get on with it!*

Even though it seemed like months, Bart and Susannah were pronounced man and wife a few moments later.

After the ceremony, friends surrounded the happy couple to offer their congratulations, not only for their new marriage, but for surviving the ceremony as well! Willie Pettit came up proudly and gave Susannah a big, welcoming hug as if she had just been inducted into a new family of gold miners who had previously included only himself and his partner in the dirt business, Bart Barrington. It was the last time either Bart or Susannah would ever see Wilderness Pettit alive. Shortly thereafter, he was found shot to death at the dig, gunned down in cold blood. With the deputizing and prompt action of a makeshift posse (which included the lawlessness-scalding Damascus Gulch), the killers were tracked down and apprehended.

It was King and his gang of claim-stake thieves.

Without a trial (the evidence of guilt was overwhelming, and the townspeople wanted the churlish King and his vermin bandits' sporadic reign of terror to be finished once and for all), they were all summarily strung up in the center of town, one by one, from the same tree that had claimed the life of Curtis Calhoun. The dandelion preacher-turned-poacher did not give a chance for any last words from the condemned. He offered his own instead. Branding these "pestilential minions of darkness" with the mark of Cain so efficiently that they would be ushered into Hades without so much as a request for positive identification.

The only encouraging news swirling around the very sad funeral of Wilderness Pettit was that a fecund Susannah Barrington was with child. While his wife took things very slowly in the new house they had built next to the parsonage, Bart continued to work the lucrative hole in the ground up on the mountainside that had reverted back to him after Willie's untimely death. Sometimes he and Obsidian were gone for days at a time, which did not sit well with Susannah. For Bart, it was unnerving at first, to be digging at the very location of his friend's murder. But he felt assured that the assailants had been thoroughly swept from the Earth. Eventually, Bart exhausted what the dirt had to give forth. Bart Barrington had been one of the rare folks to have amassed enough money for a lifetime. He returned to Hang Town, permanently, having sold his claim to a new prospector just into town who had enough fresh-off-the-boat-strike-it-rich optimism to deflect Bart's assurances that all of the hole's potential gold had been removed.

It was only a few weeks after Bart permanently moved back into town that Chance Barrington was born in April 1852. Chance was a very big baby, which made Susannah's labor strenuous. The church midwives had their work cut out for them as they at once tried to soothe the mother from her pain and coax the crowning son into the world. Chance was bright and cheery from his very first days. He was the delight of his mother, father, and caustic grandfather, who, for the next ten years, poured the molten liquid of his biblical heritage into his bouncing, pudgy grandson. Susannah also introduced her son to her own kinder, gentler Heavenly Father. Bart's pithy contribution to Chance's spiritual upbringing came directly from his mother.

"Character. Have one. Judge one."

Chance's sister, Amanda, was born five years later. Susannah's labor for her daughter was not nearly as agonizing, nor was Amanda's relationship with her grandfather nearly as motivated. It seemed that Damascus had more of a natural affinity toward the boy; the little girl made him uncomfortable. His wife, Missy, had borne the brunt of raising Susannah, as Damascus was either sequestered in his study fortifying his sermon for the next Sunday, or visiting someone from his former congregation in Chicago, or on the street corner "preachin' to the passersby," inveighing against their sin right on the spot.

He had not experienced much hands-on training in raising girls. Since Missy had died when Susannah was 17, he had missed her childhood upbringing entirely. Little Amanda's arrival had rewound the clock back to those preoccupied days of absentee fathering and had left Damascus uncomfortable with his past failures and present inadequacies.

On the other hand, he maintained his natural bent toward Chance, who was all boy. While the country was teetering toward its own Civil War, they would work and play side by side at every opportunity: hunting, fishing, debating, Chance calling his mentor "Grandpa Cuss" from a very young age.

Both Bart and Susannah saw the discrepancy in the attentions of Damascus early on and worked tirelessly in trying to bond the stilted relationship between grandfather and granddaughter. Their sincere efforts were tragically aborted, however, when, in 1863, a decisive bullet claimed the life of Damascus Gulch once and for all. The culprit was never discovered. Damascus was cut down while walking in broad daylight to the General Store. He had made many spiritual enemies, what with his constant haranguing over all things sinful, so his violent death was seen by the townsfolk as an expected reverberation of his antagonistic sermons over so many years. All were confident, however, that Damascus would elbow his way right into Abraham's bosom, edging out Lazarus and bumping him to the floor, where Cuss could have a clear view of "Purgatory" far below and could cat-call from the eternal safety of the Patriarch's lap at those iniquitous souls predestined for hellfire and damnation—getting the hot and thirsty eternity they so deserved.

Susannah made sure that her father's favorite verse from 2 Thessalonians was carved on his tomb protruding above the other headstones and crosses, a regiment planted in formation behind the church accounting for so many that had been taken from loved ones and placed safely in the arms of Jesus.

"The Lord shall consume [the wicked] with the spirit of his mouth, and shall destroy with the brightness of His coming."

Not exactly comforting eulogy material, thought Bart. But a perfect summation carved in effigy for the black-and-white life lived by his father-in-law, Damascus Gulch, God's flare.

Some months after the death of her father, Susannah approached Bart with the idea of moving on. South. Bart's odd jobs around town kept him busy enough, but a feeling of wanderlust had begun to affect him as well. The waning years of the California Gold Rush had reduced the once wild and wooly Hang Town into a stagnant testimony of bygone days. Even the name had been changed to the more peaceful "Placerville" ten years earlier, in 1854. Homes and businesses were being deserted with more and more frequency as populations moved east to money-making minerals in neighboring Nevada. Even the congregation of the Placerville church, now under the antithetically gentler hand of appropriately named human cherub Wilbur Meeks, was sheltering an ever-diminishing membership. So, in the Spring of 1864, the Barringtons packed up their belongings in their wagon, and, slowly led by an aging Obsidian, headed south down the dusty road, the rustic backbone of the teenaged State of California, Highway 49.

After a few nights under the stars, Susannah coaxed her husband to let them stay a few days in a real hotel. They certainly could afford it! They stopped at Murphys and put up in the Sperry and Perry Hotel, which a decade later would gain the distinction of being the location where the notorious Black Bart would be engaged in a shootout that would riddle the hotel's front door with tourist-attractive bullet holes.

After a few days' rest, with real baths and real beds, the family pulled up their luxurious stakes and once again headed south. At the south fork of the American River, Bart marveled while standing at the whitewater's edge that this turbulent waterway, further upstream to the north at Sutter's Mill in Coloma, was the scene of that first discovery of gold that sent shockwaves of dollar signs across an impoverished and politically beleaguered globe and changed his life in Boston forever.

Their little caravan ended up in Angel's Camp, another ghost of a town still reeling from the glory days when the settlement was bustling with 49ers. They lingered here much longer than Bart would have desired. After many discussions late into the night, Susannah and Bart finally agreed upon burgeoning Los Angeles as their ultimate destination. This would afford Chance and Amanda every opportunity in friendships, education, and careers. Even though the family was well-to-do by most standards, Bart insisted that the children have the opportunity to work for themselves. Their fulfillment would be based on the sweat of their brows, and not the unique flash-in-the-pan that was Bart's rare experience in the gold fields 15 years earlier.

One warm evening, when nature sang that she was indeed on the cusp of summer, a crowd had gathered in a nearby field. This was a magnet for the ever-curious Chance Barrington. The crowd was surrounding a white-haired man, reminiscent of his own grandfather . . . but this gentleman wore a white waistcoat. As Chance drew closer, he could hear the man speaking through the clenched teeth required to hold his smoking cigar in place. He blew a puff and then, with practiced panache, deftly extracted the cigar with his thumb and index finger to give more room for the articulate yarn-spinning yet to come.

From where he stood on a cask (molasses or something), in order to get a better view of the stranger, Chance was mesmerized, though he was able to hear only fragments of the stranger's recitations from the outskirts of the crowd. He caught whimsical and wondrous bits and pieces about frogs and jumping contests, which were augmented by bursts of uproarious laughter from the riveted bystanders. Chance burst into the family camp over an hour later and told his worried mother about the stranger and his wild stories. He was promised that, if he finished his schoolwork (that Susannah had dutifully assigned to both Chance and Amanda) and chores around their camp, he could return the next evening and see if the gentleman was once again entertaining the Angel's Camp townsfolk.

For three nights, Chance would routinely search for the whereabouts of the man whom they say lived up on Jackass Hill, seventeen miles southeast of town, and elbow his way through the throng that had gathered at storefront, boardwalk, or open field, to be in the best position to hear the tall tales of this vest-popping raconteur from the East.

Tales of steamboats and mighty rivers, gold mining, adventuresome travels to exotic foreign lands, even hilarious speeches about God and the Bible! Chance barreled into the family tent on their last night in town and exclaimed to his mother, "If only the Bible had been written like that man talked, why, the churches would be packed!" He then proceeded to repeat some of the stories he had heard that night. Bart, Susannah, and Amanda sat attentively while Chance did his level best to imitate the snake-charming, crowd-pleasing wiles of Samuel Langhorne Clemens, alias Mark Twain. Susannah, however, bit her lip at the scriptural liberties that had been implanted in her beloved son. But she marveled at how precisely and colorfully Chance could repeat a story. Soon he was telling stories of his own, from Angel's Camp through Columbia, Jamestown, and Chinese Camp, all the way to the City of the Angels!

After a few weeks upon arriving in Los Angeles, and with Gold Rush cash in hand, the Barrington family rented a room above a grocery store and settled into their new, temporary home. As the Barringtons were well-to-do, Bart again resigned himself to odd jobs around town just to keep himself occupied. He made sure his son Chance was also gainfully employed as a clerk in the grocery store below their home, which could be fitted around his mother's home-schooling schedule.

It was not long after their arrival that Bart was wired news of his beloved mother's graduating to glory. At his request, the family attorney liquidated the Barrington assets in Boston, and Bart's personal coffers were further endowed with new money, this time heavy with the emotion of loss. This familial void was compounded with the death of his trusty horse, Obsidian. "The trip must have been too much for him," said Bart when he discovered his long-time, faithful companion dead in the stall Bart had rented in a nearby stable. He thought of Missy Gulch and her succumbing to the very same fate after the rigors of travel had overwhelmed her soul as well. This succeeded in severely tainting the family's first impressions of the bustling Los Angeles. Bart was not sure the four of them would be able to climb out of the deep hole the temptation to go back to "Placerville" had dug.

However, Bart happened to meet up with one Prudent Beaudry and struck up a conversation about the irresistible real estate market in Southern California. Prudent assured Bart that it was on the brink of booming. With his Gold Rush and inheritance savings, Bart secured a nice piece of property from Mr. Beaudry, in an area known as Bunker Hill, and was soon enmeshed as an adjunct general contractor overseeing the building of their lavish, three-story Victorian estate whose wraparound porch, a portico moat, was the envy of the developing new neighborhood.

Susannah Gulch Barrington kept a keen eye on her son and daughter, and made sure their social life was well-orchestrated. Since they were not enrolled in any public school, she was strict on the entire family's attending the Community Church of Los Angeles. It was there that Chance Barrington first caught sight of the voluptuous, yet conservative Cordelia Walsh. Fueled by one church social after another, Chance and Cordelia struck up an endearing romance, which led to their marriage late in 1880. Since the Barrington house was so large (looming as it did upon the hill with a breathless view of the surrounding Los Angeles basin), Chance and Cordelia moved in with the rest of the family. With so much available space and freedom to roam upstairs, they rarely saw the other members of the Barrington household. This cordon of privacy that seemingly unlimited square footage had allowed might have been a contributing factor to the announcement of the pregnancy of Cordelia Barrington and the arrival of their son Frank Barrington nine months later in January 1882.

Prudent Beaudry's real estate predictions had proven correct, and the commercial and business development of Bunker Hill exploded. Like his gold-giving hole up above Placerville, Bart had been on the ground floor of many lucrative business investments. Thanks to tips from Prudent, his attraction to the buzzing real-estate world became his very own obsession. Bart's insatiable appetite was passed on directly to his son, Chance, and Chance's to his son, Frank. It was a package deal, however, for, along with his business sensibilities, in the oral tradition of the gospel writers of old, Chance also poured into his boy a great deal of his storytelling talent.

Regretfully, appreciation and implementation of this trait seemed to be lost on the ever-pragmatic, unimaginative Frank Barrington.

One day a few years after the turn of the century, Chance and his junior real-estate partner Frank were taking the one-minute ride up Angel's Flight, "the shortest railway in the World," for a penny apiece, back to their home on top of Bunker Hill, when

20-year-old Frank mentioned to his father that he desired to set out on his own. After careful research, and wise counsel from Prudent Beaudry, Frank set his sights upon a beautiful, idyllic community nestled in the Sierra Nevada foothills some 25 miles to the east of Los Angeles, Vista Pacifica. The town was growing rapidly, and they, too, boasted of their own cable-car system, "The Funicular," that took folks from the bottom of the hill to the top for five cents apiece. Frank purchased a piece of property commanding an excellent view of the mountainside and began building his own Victorian mansion. His mother, Cordelia, still invoked her maternal prowess on her single son. She took their horse and buggy on the long journey around the Hollywood Hills to Vista Pacifica as often as possible not only to see how the great new home was coming along, but also to scan the local female landscape of the little community for any marriageable prospects for her handsome, skinny offspring. As there was only one little church in the town, her search for a "nice Christian girl" was challenging. But while Frank was busy checking on inventories of glass, lumber, and pipes, or directing carpenters, plumbers, and assorted craftsmen, Cordelia Barrington was combing the mountainside for his prospective wife. "It was just like a betrothal from medieval times!" Frank would later say at family gatherings about his wife, Katherine, while glaring at his wily mother. Cordelia Barrington would sit back, sipping her tea, basking in her accomplishment of her son's marriage to the beautiful Katherine in 1903. But she didn't stop there. Every visit she and Chance made to Vista Pacifica included a hard look at the midsection of her new daughter-in-law, to see if perchance there was a grandchild in the works. To her dismay, the wait would be a long one.

After marrying off his little sister, Amanda (who would eventually find herself divorced twice over from two hasty, unsound selections plucked from the available man pool), sadly burying his beloved father and mother, and considering the sky-rocketing value of their property, Chance Barrington decided to sell their palatial home on Bunker Hill to one of the highest-bidding hotels that were among the many businesses salivating over the predominantly commercial area. During the negotiations, Chance told his son a heartwarming "story" about how he and Frank's mother were graciously allowed to enjoy life upstairs in the family home on Bunker Hill for as long as they wished. They were always welcome. Only this time, Aesop did not offer any moral to the story; there was no dangling of a tempting "long life" promise for honoring your father and mother. Chance floated his little "story" only in front of Frank, appealing to his sensitivities to provide a realistic ending. He agreed. So, family history repeated itself as Chance and Cordelia Barrington occupied the upstairs portion of the home of Frank and Katherine in Vista Pacifica. Since this home (which also included a wraparound porch that was the envy of the young neighborhood at the bottom of the hill) was enormous as well, there was no sense of overcrowding, and bumping into one another had to be with intent. But because Chance was so large, his upstairs footfalls overhead pounded the ceiling and shook the expensive chandeliers underneath on a regular basis. Creaking floorboards and swaying light fixtures were a common occurrence in the Barrington household.

After seven long years, to the delight of meddlesome Cordelia, Katherine finally made the announcement that she was going to have a baby. This was greeted by exultant squeals of jubilant celebration. But the squeals turned into blood-curdling screams nine months later as Katherine labored long and hard to give birth to her very large son, Sidney.

According to his grandfather and grandmother, their jolly grandson Sidney would enjoy a childhood throughout a most propitious and challenging time. During his growing-up years, the likes of Cecil B. DeMille and D.W. Griffith would cause the movie industry to explode in nearby Hollywood, which would spill over into neighboring communities, including Vista Pacifica. As a result, Cordelia Barrington (who gave Sidney his first, illustrated *King James Bible* when he was six years old) would say that she was "pleased as punch" that the God-fearing citizens decided to finally build a nice, large brick church at the base of the mountainside from which to combat and vanquish from its briny battlements the worldly influences of motion-picture celluloid that was flickering up on the silver screen. Conveniently, she never mentioned the enormous Arabian eyesore being carved right above her beloved future sanctuary—a Tinsel Town tribute in effigy to her worst cultural fears. But her silence spoke volumes, loud and clear.

"Now this town will have something worthwhile to offer the world," she would say with great satisfaction, "when Jesus's juggernaut is properly standing guard up on that hill." And she would march about proudly spouting the Apostle Paul's two-pronged question that was anything but rhetorical,

"And how shall they believe in Him of whom they have not heard? And how shall they hear without a preacher?"

This particular church would be an institution to which she gave generously (and anonymously, under the alias of Alma Davenport, a widow) until the day she died. She also insisted that her one grandson would attend the only church in town.

(Her eternal rest on the "other side" in glory would still be very sweet three decades later—if there were decades where she was resting—as her special grandson would be classified 4-F by the United States Armed Forces. Due to his misshapen foot arches, neither of which would ever be fully corrected as more and more weight would be added over the years to complicate their duty of motion, Sidney would be provided with an uninterrupted four years of attendance at a midwest Bible college. He would return to Our Father's Evangelical Church to become one of the most influential Bible teachers ever to waddle through the halls of its Educational Christianity building. Hundreds of kids would benefit from this, his real job, he would say. He sold real estate on the side merely to make a living, so he could make a difference.)

Even with the depletion of the local manpower during World War I, industries grew exponentially to fund the national efforts overseas, which gave the town a shot in the arm of prosperity. And then one historic day a few years later, an unknown young sculptor took up residence and proceeded to carve up the mountainside, which gave their town, like Placerville, a brand-new name.

One night after a special dinner celebrating Grandma Cordelia's 73rd birthday, the ever-broadening Chance and Sidney were especially "stuffed to the gills" and decided to take in the cool night breezes. They lumbered out onto the sprawling front porch and simultaneously plopped into the swing, giving every link of the supporting chains a run for their money after being so strenuously stretched. The swing creaked and groaned under the combined weight of the two portly men as they both sipped tall glasses of iced tea and looked out at the half-finished head of Rudolph Valentino in the distance. The granite face was mysteriously luminescent in the waning western light. They also watched the blinking red lights of "The Funicular" slowly creeping its way up Valentino Avenue—a 5-cent ride they had taken together many times when Sidney was a child, "just for the heck of it," his grandpa would say.

As if he knew his time was growing short (he would die a few weeks later), 75-year-old Chance Barrington decided that this was a mighty fine moment to bestow some pearls of wisdom upon his impressionable 17-year-old grandson, now a Junior at Monument High School, with a feisty new Italian girlfriend. Looking straight ahead, he cleared his throat. "Ya know, son, in their twilight years, Adam and Eve was probably sittin' on a porch much like this one well into their 900s. They were rockin' back 'n forth in their chairs, lookin' out at a world gone to pot; wars, poverty, immorality, injustice, avarice, greed, even their own kids killin' each other. All because of a wrong decision they had made almost a millennium before with that sneakin' serpent." He paused and then slapped his large hand upon Sidney's equally large knee and said, abruptly,

"Character. Have one. Judge one."

"Huh?" responded the teenage Sidney, looking up at his grandfather curiously over the rim of his iced-tea glass.

Chance Barrington looked into the eyes of his grandson, sighed, and looked once again out yonder at the carved head in the distant mountainside. He felt the gnawing necessity to make his point, and to make it right. Perhaps the Bible still might be of some use right about now. "An example out of Jonah," he concluded. He pulled out a cigar and lit it. After blowing out a puffy white cloud of smoke, he smoothly pulled the cigar out of his mouth with his thumb and index finger, and leaned back into the swing, putting his large, booted feet up on the porch railing.

"Son, maybe it'd be clearer for you if I was to tell you a little story of character gone fishin'." As Chance spoke these cryptic words, a puzzled Sidney sat on the edge of the swing, this generation hanging upon his grandfather's every word.

"A land mammal becomes a water rat while trying to outfox the Top Dog into using another guinea pig. Something smells fishy in the kangaroo court because the slothful scaredy-cat tries to weasel his way out of the doghouse. The king of beasts ferrets out the lion's share of the truth as the stubborn mule worms his way into confessing his bird-brained scheme that he doesn't want to be the gopher that gives snakes-in-the-grass bear hugs."

EPILOGUE

On a Friday at dusk in August 2004, what seemed like the entire City of Monument gathered in the grandstands for the sunset dedication ceremony of the completed Rudolph Valentino. Press corps from more than 50 newspapers had descended upon every available space along the base of the mountain to thoroughly record this one-of-a-kind, "Facial Festivus." Television vans, lights, cameras, technicians, grips, food trucks, and roving reporters hurriedly seeking spontaneous interviews while being dabbed and combed from behind by frenzied makeup artists, all adding to the media blitz milieu that was this frenetic afternoon. Along with most of our major business establishments, I closed the Block Insurance Agency early so my employees and I could scramble up the hillside and get a decent seat in the grandstands erected especially for the occasion. I met Maria, Sharayah, and Samantha who, after what was thought to be a very preemptive, early arrival, had secured only a four-person space on the very back row of the bleachers with the other proletariat! We could not even sit next to my parents, who were seated a few rows forward to the right (they had used the occasion once again as an excuse for another "forsaking the gathering" break from their church, and tripped southward), along with Owen, Penny, and Owen Jr., who was whacking the kid next to him with a half-eaten cotton candy stick. We squeezed next to the entire Holbert family on our right and Frank Petry on our left.

When I had caught my breath from the death-defying fancy footwork and precise-equilibrium negotiations required to adroitly stair-step my way up the grandstands through multiple rows of wall-to-wall people, all the while trying to say "hello" courteously enough to everyone I knew (without spilling their drinks or paper trays of food), and straddling over ducking heads, keeping my balance with the help of an occasional unsolicited shoulder, I finally plopped down, quite winded, next to Maria and was able to take in the sea of familiar heads (even from the back) that packed the grandstands this evening.

It was with the deepest regret that Esmeralda Bertuccio Barrington could not be on hand to witness this auspicious and momentous occasion.

She had passed away a few months before at the age of 92, a full 17 years after the death of her beloved Sid Barrington. Her passing was earlier than anticipated, as if God had spared her from being enveloped in a final fog of last days' forgetfulness.

She was buried on a beautiful Spring day at Forest Lawn Hollywood Hills, next to her late husband. The funeral drew a much smaller crowd than had been present at Sid Barrington's service. Death, relocations, and that relentless rampage known as the passage of time had severely thinned the ranks of mourners. But the Forty-something Musketeers, however miraculously, were all present and accounted for: Nathan Raab, Patrick Hamilton, Kenneth Ball, and myself. We gathered somberly around the graveside while Pastor Roland Jeffries gave a sweet but uninformed eulogy on behalf of this most influential of childless matriarchs.

We closed the service by singing one of Esmeralda's favorite hymns,

"My hope is built on nothing less
than Jesus' blood and righteousness.
I dare not trust the sweetest frame,
but wholly lean on Jesus' name.
On Christ the solid rock I stand."

Epilogue

It was a shame that she could not be here to witness the Rudolph Valentino dedication. Maria and I had talked with Esmeralda of our plans for taking her with us to the ceremony for weeks before she died.

We seemed to be diving into another wave of deaths lately. Only last week I received word that Annabelle Levine was now a widow and sole manager of the Cheyenne Christian Conference Center. Her husband, Fred "Fess" Levine had died from advanced prostate cancer. He had been buried in a privately owned family plot on a hillside at the camp, commanding a magnificent view of the lake below, right next to Fred's beloved, much-older sister, Cheyenne, for whom the camp was named.

The band from Monument High School played a stirring Sousa march and then broke into some unusual Arab themes. Some people were dressed up in all manner of Arab outfits, while others masqueraded as lookalikes of Charlie Chaplin, Greta Garbo, Laurel and Hardy, Marilyn Monroe, W.C. Fields, and the Marx Brothers. Colorful programs of the history of the carving were sold for ten dollars each, the proceeds going to the future upkeep of the monument by the City, so that its attempted covering by Mother Nature would forever be held in check.

As the sun was beginning to set over the Hollywood Hills to the west, our bumbling, bushy-mustachioed, dullard of a mayor Calvin Ross took to the podium while the Monument High School band played "Hail to the Chief" for the expected ceremonial pontificating and prognostication. As dandified as a coxcomb, he was also a very round bureaucrat, an honors graduate from the Sid Barrington school of proportions. His approach to the bunting-shrouded lectern looked like a large Christmas tree ornament rolling up to speak at us. The ineffectual "Hail to the Chief" fizzled rather sloppily as the ornament cleared his throat.

"Good evening, members of the City Council, distinguished guests, ladies and gentlemen, boys and girls. Eighty-three years ago this very month, Hollywood lost one of its most illustrious stars. He was the star of *The Sheik*, which premiered in 1921. One of the people sitting in the dark theater that day was none other than Max Stellar of Grand Rapids, Wisconsin . . . uh . . . Michigan! He was so moved by the picture that he began to dream of carving the face of Rudolph Valentino. He began the realization of that dream on the mountain behind me."

Like the rotation of a planet, Mayor Ross twisted his corpulent body around to look up behind him, which was no easy trick. He then reversed the revolution and returned to face us, clearing his throat a second time.

"Sadly, just like his subject, Mr. Stellar died five years after starting the project. Mr. Valentino also died five years after starring in *The Sheik* at the age of thirty-one. We here in Monument, thanks to the vision of Max Stellar, have something of which to be very proud. A fulcrum, if you will, from which our great community has always grown and prospered."

"Fulcrum? Who is his speechwriter?" whispered a curious Maria to me. But I just shook my head as the ornament orated onward.

"In 1772, when Cabrillo landed here and began his expedition eastward . . ." he paused to think, looking skyward and putting a finger to his billowy chin, he mumbled offhandedly but still loudly enough to be picked up by the microphone ". . . or was it Cortez? Anyway, when they landed here and discovered this beautiful valley, they would have no idea that here was . . ."

Mayor Ross's glib, long-winded bloviating blew my wandering mind almost as far back in time as his speech reached, to a synopsis I had breathed into life from the 23rd Chapter of the Book of Acts,

"As soon as the black-and-white checkered flag was waved back and forth in the temple courtyard, the annual Sanhedrin Hot Air Balloon Race was on! Crowds of healthy-lunged High Priests from both the Team Pharisee and Team Sadducee sects had gathered around each competing basket under the open end of the gigantic, deflated balloons and began talking up a storm at each other, spouting the tedious religious laws, ordinances, creeds, and worldviews for which they were both famous: Whether you can pick heads of grain on the Sabbath. What is the greatest Commandment? and maliciously poking each other while asking if they were the Son of God. Before long, the large hot-air balloons of Team Pharisee began filling up and were bobbing in the cool breezes, straining against the ropes that held them to the ground. Pre-selected, lightweight members of Team Pharisee jumped into each basket, quickly cutting the restraining ropes while tossing out the sandbags, and the balloons sailed high into the bright Jerusalem sky, Team Pharisee winning the hot-air competition for another consecutive year. The members of Team Sadducee were still talking at each other, trying in vain to inflate their balloons, which were still spread out limply on the hot stone-courtyard pavement. They would not listen to the event officials who came over and tried to explain to Team Sadducee for the umpteenth time that their balloons never got off the ground because they did not believe that anything could be raised up."

Mayor Ross waxed eloquent for a good hour, walking his citizens through our town's colorful history as he could best remember it, beginning with a convoluted Spanish root system and the first name of our breathtaking little hamlet, "Vista Pacifica."

As planned, his turgid speech finally concluded in darkness. "And now, citizens of Monument," said Mayor Ross as he spread out his arms magnanimously, "please stand and join me in welcoming back the completed dream of Max Stellar. From his 1921 classic, *The Sheik*, I give you . . . RUDOLPH VALENTINO!"

With that, he pulled a switch at the podium, and five gigantic floodlights stationed along Ridgeway Avenue came to life, flashing quintet beams of light onto the completed 100-foot head in all its freshly chiseled grandeur. Another five searchlights began sweeping back and forth across the blackened sky beyond, looking to neighboring cities for miles around like we were hosting a star-studded movie premier gala at Grauman's Chinese Theatre. The Monument High School band played "Hooray for Hollywood," while exploding red, white, and blue fireworks burst and spangled the vacant, awaiting canopy above.

From my high vantage point at the top of the grandstands, I turned around and looked straight down the center of Valentino Avenue. The pavement was now a heavenly street of gold, aglow in the wash of the twinkling white lights that lit the rows of trees along the grass center divide that traced the old route of "The Funicular" and those on the parkways lining both sides of the Avenue as well. It looked like the nests of thousands of firefly squadrons. Far below, at the bottom of the hill, was the spectator-slowing-congested freeway, whose headlights and brake lights moved like white and red lava in opposite directions.

Our city never looked better, I thought to myself, voicing three generations of built-up civic pride. I turned around and looked to my left at Our Father's Evangelical Church, illuminated as well with its usual, subtle night lighting. The gothic, unassailable brick building seemed to be simply watching quietly, calm, serene, and strong, without reaction or fanfare, over just another earthly milestone. Majestic as an army with banners.

"And neither has our church!" I added, audibly voicing to myself the spiritual call, strength, and hope of 50 generations.

The grandstands thundered with the clapping and stomping to the august music. Glow sticks, passed out to the children for the occasion, sprang up from the audience like hundreds of dancing batons. "This rocks!" yelled Samantha, while she twirled two glowing red and blue batons over her head and stomped as hard as she could upon the feeble, weakening planking of the grandstands. There was laughter, cheers, festal shouts, and even a few tears daubed well into the night at the "monumental" milestone we had reached together as a community. I could even feel a lump in my own throat, standing there on the highest bleacher, my own little Mount Nebo, next to Maria, Sharayah, and Samantha, as I looked up at the gargantuan, handsome movie star that had be-knighted our little town with a brand-new name eight decades earlier, changing its destiny forever. Fireworks booming, car horns honking, whistles tweeting from the crowd-controlling constabulary; for years to come, every citizen of Monument would say unequivocally that this bench-mark evening in August 2004 was one of the most sublime, memorable spectacles they had ever seen in his or her lifetime.

That night, I went to bed with my recapping mind whirring from the events of the past couple of hours, carving them indelibly, just like on our mountainside, into the permanent bank of my memory. The next morning, at a digital 6:36 a.m., the still-idling RPMs of my brain waves awoke my obeisant body earlier than expected with a clever agenda. In response, I quietly slipped out of bed and tiptoed down the stairs. I plopped down on the living room couch. Now, before anyone upstairs was awake, I had precious time to open the final pages of Milton Derringer's opus.

"They had disappeared as quickly as they had come. The little country had been given a respite, a second chance to not only trace its heritage—when giants of a new republic

had roamed the earth—but to meet it face to face, to hear directly from their forefathers the reasons for the foundations firmly underfoot. The Father had once again shed His grace upon the land with a purely educational phenomenon. Now would come the test: Would the country scrape off the topsoil and residue of present-day, progressive thinking? This would be their final exam. The next time the Father came calling, it would be apocalyptic. No warnings. All of the signs in place. Trumpets would sound, and school would be out . . . forever. History would not repeat itself. Until then, the country had been given all the precious time left in heaven's storehouses to mull things over.

"If my people, who are called by my name,"

"IAN, I'M READY TO PAINT THE CEILING!"
I jolted upright at the unexpected call from upstairs in Samantha's room.
"IAN?"

"will humble themselves"

I let go a painful sigh.
"Do we have to do this right now?" I yelled back. *Keep reading, Ian.*

"and pray and seek my face"

Please God, not right now.
"YES, HONEY. IT'S TIME!"

"and turn from their wicked ways,"

"I'm kinda busy right now!" *Keep reading, Ian.*

"then I will hear from heaven"

"DOING WHAT? READING?"
A second sigh. "Just a minute!" I yelled. *Keep reading, Ian.*

"and will forgive their sin and heal their land.
2 Chronicles 7:14
THE END"

"I'M ROLLING!"
"I'm coming!"

THE END

About the Author

B rad Brown graduated with high honors with a Master's degree in Theology from Talbot School of Theology in La Mirada, California. He also graduated cum laude from Biola University with a degree in Speech Communication and a minor degree in Biblical Studies and Theology. He was voted the Most Outstanding Student of the Speech Communication Department for 1981–1982. *Upon This Rock.* is preceded by *This Is The Church . . .* , and *Rightly Dividing?* and is followed by *Raised!*—the completed four "seasons" of Our Father's Evangelical Church.

Brad lives with his wife Cindy in Franktown, Colorado.